THE *Temple*
OUR HOME
AWAY
FROM HOME

THE Temple
OUR HOME AWAY FROM HOME

ARDETH G. KAPP

DESERET BOOK
SALT LAKE CITY, UTAH

Cover illustration by Doug Corbett

Library of Congress Cataloging-in-Publication Data

    Kapp, Ardeth Greene, 1931-
      The temple, our home away from home / Ardeth Greene Kapp.
         p.   cm.
    Includes index.
    ISBN 1-57008-910-8 (alk. paper)
      1. Christian life—Mormon authors.   2. Meditations.   3. Mormon
temples. I. Title.
    BX8656.K395   2003
    248.4'89332—dc21
                                     2002155957

Printed in the United States of America   72076-6966
Publishers Printing, Salt Lake City, Utah

10   9   8   7   6   5   4   3   2   1

CONTENTS

INTRODUCTION

*M*y cousin Colleen and I shared many experiences growing up just through the open field from each other. The only real conflict we had was the ever-continuing debate about whose dad's cows were the best. She stood on the firm conviction that her dad's Holstein cows gave the most milk. I did not argue that point but defended with equal conviction the notion that my dad's Jersey cows gave the richest and therefore the best milk, making them the best cows. To this day, in memory of our childhood, we are still exchanging evidence to support our claims, although I am not nearly as sure on that issue as I once was. But there is another matter that first arose in that same setting in our young lives upon which I stand absolutely, undeniably sure.

There is a resurrection.

It was springtime. The lilac bushes were in full bloom, filling the air with a sweet aroma, when I had my first experience with the sadness of death. Colleen and I were sorrowing. We had made a little coverlet to wrap around the tiny dead bird, a meadowlark that had frequented our trees in recent weeks. We tucked it into a matchbox coffin to be placed in its final resting place under the maple tree by the lilac bush.

My Aunt Lavern, Colleen's mother, often sang at funerals in our small town. It seemed to us only fitting that the occasion of a life ended should have the respect of the song she always sang at such events. She was standing at the kitchen window; we beckoned to her to come. She left her bread-making, still wearing her apron with wisps of flour down the front, and joined us in response to our earnest request. As if there were a full audience like the ones she was used to when she gave it her best, Aunt Lavern sang in a deep, melancholy tone from the largo of the *New World Symphony*, by Anton Dvorak, "Goin' home, goin' home, I'm a-goin' home." She sang all the verses while two little girls with bowed heads mourned the passing of a tiny bird.

With the matchbox placed in the shallow grave and covered over, and our memorial service ended, I knew in my young mind that our little bird would not remain in that matchbox in the ground. It would be taken back home, where it would spread its wings and fly again.

It was under a lilac bush at the funeral service of a bird that I first experienced these feelings of eternity. I didn't understand at that time about the separation of body and spirit, or the doctrines of resurrection and exaltation, but I knew in my heart that this was not the end. *And if Heavenly Father cares for even a bird,* I have thought since then, *what will it be like when we all return home?*

Over the years I have come to realize more fully, "by study and also by faith" (D&C 88:118), that this earth life is not our final home: not for the birds, not for the lilac bushes, not for us, not for any living thing. "For notwithstanding they die, they also shall rise again, a spiritual body" (D&C 88:27).

We are away from home in a strange place. We have not traveled this way before, and there is much opposition during these perilous times that puts at risk our safe return. The very purpose of this life is to be "tried in all things" (D&C 136:31). President Spencer W. Kimball, who experienced so many trials in his life, expressed his belief: "I am positive in my mind that the Lord has planned our destiny. Sometime we'll understand fully, and when we see back from the vantage point of the future, we shall be satisfied with many of the happenings of this life that are so difficult for us to comprehend" (*Faith Precedes the Miracle* [Salt Lake City: Deseret Book, 1972], 105).

The veil that was drawn when we entered this earth life dims the memory that we lived in our Father's presence. Is it any wonder that we should experience on occasion a sense of homesickness that we can't really explain? Have you noticed how many times in the scriptures we are counseled to "remember, remember." Alma, speaking to his son Helaman, repeats over and over, "O remember, remember, my son" (Alma 37:13). Later, Helaman repeats the counsel to his own sons, Nephi and Lehi: "Now, my sons, remember, remember" (Helaman 5:12).

Remembering implies that there had to be a previous learning, which there was. This life is not the beginning.

In a vision given to President Joseph F. Smith now known as section 138 of the Doctrine and Covenants, we learn of many great leaders and other choice spirits who were to take part in this vital latter-day work: "*Even before they were born, they, with many others, received their first lessons in the world of spirits and were prepared to come forth in the due time of the*

Lord to labor in his vineyard for the salvation of the souls of men" (D&C 138:56; emphasis added). This is our time.

It is in and through our covenant relationship with the Lord Jesus Christ that we prepare to feel and know and remember things we may not be able to explain but cannot deny. We can experience regular communication and encouragement from Home. President Joseph F. Smith teaches of how we awaken to truths through the power of the Spirit: "All those salient truths which come home so forcibly to the head and heart seem but the awakening of the memories of the spirit. Can we know anything here that we did not know before we came? Are not the means of knowledge in the first estate equal to those of this?" (*Gospel Doctrine*, 5th ed. [Salt Lake City: Deseret Book, 1939], 13).

The more aware we become that the spirit world is an extension of our mortal existence, the better prepared we are to set aside the treasures of this world and establish priorities in relation to the next. The temple is the bridge between mortality and immortality. It is the place where we receive comfort, peace, vision, hope, and promise. In the temple we are reminded of our identity—who we are and who we are to become—and we prepare to fulfill our foreordained mission.

The temple is a place of revelation where we learn to hear the promptings of the Spirit. Here we learn of the purpose of life and the profound blessings of eternal life. Everything associated with the temple points to Christ and our covenant relationship with him.

Through ordinances available only in the temple, we are strengthened in our ability to live in the world without being overcome by the vicissitudes of the world. From the writings of President Joseph Fielding Smith we learn of what we might expect: "If we go into the temple, we raise our hands and covenant that we will serve the Lord and observe his commandments and keep ourselves unspotted from the world. If we realize what we are doing, then the endowment, the covenant will be a protection to us all our lives—a protection, which a man who does not go to the temple does not have.

"I have heard my father say that in the hours of temptation he would think of the promises, the covenants that he made in the House of the Lord, and they were a protection to him. . . . This protection is what these ceremonies are for, in part. They save us now and exalt us hereafter, if we will honor them. I know that this protection is given, for I too have realized it, as have thousands of others who remember their obligation" (*Take Heed to Yourselves* [Salt Lake City: Deseret Book, 1966], 119).

Now, we need to realize that as we return to the temple again and again with a strong desire to have revealed to us the will of our Father in Heaven, we may not always receive clear and specific answers. The answers, when they come, may not be on our timeline or according to our deepest desires. However, as we learn to wait upon the Lord—whatever our heartache, disappointment, or discouragement—we can know that our Heavenly Father knows and loves each of us individually.

I testify that he knows our struggles and triumphs, our greatest joys and deepest sorrows. I have not seen his face, but I have been in his house and have felt his presence and can bear witness of his concern for each of his children. It is my hope that, in reading the pages of this book, you will feel an increased desire to be drawn more frequently to that environment away from the world, that you might be enveloped in the blessings that await in our home away from home.

1

AWAY FROM HOME

I will never forget my first time away from home on my own. My mom and dad had sacrificed for me to go away to school, where I would be provided with opportunities that were not available in our small town. I was young and inexperienced, but it was necessary for me to leave home to get the education I needed.

On the memorable day of my departure, my grandparents and brother and sisters and friends had all wished me luck and said they would miss me and would look forward to my return. (My younger sister expressed her concern over who would mop the floor while I was away.) It was all very exciting, this great adventure, until my mom and dad said their goodbyes, embracing me and encircling me in the arms of their love. They spoke of their trust and assured me that I would do well; they would be praying for me. I was much less excited about leaving home at that moment. I wasn't sure I had learned all the lessons I needed to prepare me for the unknown.

Even today I can feel the deep and encompassing pangs of homesickness that I experienced soon after I arrived in Provo, Utah. Everything was different. I didn't know my way around. Even the style of the girls' dresses was different from what I was used to, and I didn't yet have any friends. Soon I began marking the calendar and counting the days until Christmas, when I would return safely home to the security and love of my parents and family.

I marked off the days and weeks painstakingly until the looked-for day finally came. When I crossed the U.S. border into Canada, and the customs officer asked the usual question, "What have you to declare?" I wanted to blurt out, "I'm homesick, that's what I have to declare!" About ten miles from home I could hardly restrain myself from jumping out of the car and running, knowing my family would be watching from the kitchen window, anticipating my arrival. I could already feel that warm and safe and secure feeling of being welcomed home.

Since that time I have had many occasions to be in the Salt Lake airport, observing from the sidelines the anticipation, the exquisite joy, the jubilance as families await that moment of grand reunion when their missionary son or daughter returns home having filled an honorable mission. This scene awakens an excitement deep within, an anticipation of our final homecoming, when we return after having been away at school, so to speak, having learned the lessons we could learn only by leaving home for a time.

There is within each of us a quiet longing, a feeling bone-marrow deep that draws us home. The writings of George Q. Cannon help us understand this feeling of homesickness that is so indescribable yet so real at times: "If we could understand the glory we once had with our Father in heaven, we would be discontented in dwelling in this condition of existence. We would pine for the home we left behind us. Its glory and its beauty, its heavenly graces and delights were of such a character that we would pine for it with that homesickness that men have some partial knowledge of here on earth" (*Gospel Truth* [Salt Lake City: Deseret Book, 1987], 1:8).

On the early morning of September 11, 2001, I was at the airport in Tucson, Arizona. Traveling alone, I strapped myself securely into my seat on Delta Airlines Flight 3983, departure time 6:20 A.M. I was fully anticipating arriving home on schedule, knowing that my husband, Heber, would be there to meet me. The steward welcomed everyone on board and explained that there would be a slight delay. This was not unusual, and there was no negative response from anyone. Then, a few minutes later, the steward asked—no, more like *ordered*—everyone to disembark from the plane immediately. Passengers began questioning, expressing concern over missing connecting flights. It was explained that there would be no connecting flights. All planes had been grounded. In the terminal, masses of humanity stood transfixed in front of TV monitors. No one was going home.

That terrible, unforgettable day became etched in our hearts and minds forever through heinous acts of terrorism that changed the world. News stories in the days following seemed to focus on one heartfelt concern: "Will I see my loved ones again?" Many risked their lives to rescue strangers, people they never knew, in the hope of bringing families together. Some who faced imminent death as their hijacked plane was going down recorded last-minute expressions of tender love and deepest affection. Priorities changed that day. People of all faiths, nationalities, and cultures united in prayer for themselves and for others, one large family of brothers and sisters mourning the loss of the innocent victims.

How are we to understand and carry on in the face of such evil, such tragedy in our world? President Ezra Taft Benson promised, "Let us make the temple a sacred home away from our eternal home. This temple will be a standing witness that the power of God can stay the powers of evil in our midst. . . .

"Yes, there is a power associated with the ordinances of heaven—even the power of godliness—which can and will thwart the forces of evil if we will be worthy of those sacred blessings. This community will be protected, our families will be protected, our children will be safeguarded as we live the gospel, visit the temple, and live close to the Lord" (*The Teachings of Ezra Taft Benson* [Salt Lake City: Bookcraft, 1988), 256).

We are away from home. One day we shall return. The tenderness, the exquisite joy, the reality of this divine experience we cannot yet comprehend. Elder Orson F. Whitney captured some of the feeling that may accompany our reunion with the Savior as manifested to him in a dream: "I ran [to meet the Lord] . . . , fell at his feet, clasped him around the knees, and begged him to take me with him. I shall never forget the kind and gentle manner in which he stooped, raised me up, and embraced me. It was so vivid, so real. I felt the very warmth of his body, as He held me in his arms" (*Through Memory's Halls* [Independence, Mo.: Press of Zion's Printing and Publishing Co., 1930], 83).

Brigham Young gives us another glimpse of this grand reunion: "There is no spirit but what was pure and holy when it came here from the celestial world. . . . [God] is the Father of our spirits: and if we could know, understand, and do His will, every soul would be prepared to return back to His presence. And when they get there, they would see that they had formerly lived there for ages, that they had previously been acquainted with every nook and corner, with the palaces, walks, and gardens; and they would embrace their Father, and He would embrace them and say, 'My son, my daughter, I have you home again;' and the child would say, 'O my Father, my Father, I am here again" (*Journal of Discourses*, 26 vols. [London: Latter-day Saints' Book Depot, 1854–86], 4:268).

Only in understanding eternity can we make sense of the tragedies of mortality. In the temple, as in no other place on earth, we begin to grasp the incomprehensible blessing of the atonement of Jesus Christ, which makes possible our return home. I testify that, if we will live faithful to the covenants we make there, one day we will be welcomed into his presence and encircled in the arms of his love.

A SERMON
IN THEIR SHOES

*T*here were big shoes, little shoes, tall ones, short ones—some black and some brown, some with laces and some without, all carefully placed on a two-tiered shoe rack just inside the entrance to the Cardston Alberta Temple. In this beautiful building, located at the foot of the rugged Canadian Rockies and overlooking the vast Canadian prairie, the shoe rack extends the full width of the foyer, thirty feet or more. Like Moses, who was told by the Lord on Sinai, "Put off thy shoes from off thy feet, for the place whereon thou standest is holy ground" (Exodus 3:5), patrons of the Cardston Temple have a long-standing custom of removing their shoes just inside the entrance to the Lord's house.

In a meeting with a group of newly called temple presidents and their wives, one of the speakers suggested that we consider "the sermon in their shoes." He said, "If you walk through the temple where the patrons leave their shoes, you will see testimonies in the variety of their shoes. You will see the membership of the Church in the shoes." He added, "Remember, they have just stepped out of the world into the temple."

Arriving at the Cardston Temple, where my husband and I were called to serve for three years, I was anxious to understand the sermon he referred to. Were there to be layers of meaning found in the admonition to look at the shoes, or was it simply an interesting display of a variety of footwear?

I took the first available opportunity to make some careful observations. The shoes were placed side by side, with no apparent attention to any categorizing, classifying, separating, or even noticing where one pair of shoes was placed in relation to another. Curious, I walked the full length of the entrance hall, stopping to look and ponder. I observed the high gloss of patent leather, the shoes of a lady, right next to a pair of fur-lined boots like those of a lumberman, appropriate for the weather that day. There were shoes with well-worn soles and the heels almost gone. A highly polished pair of deep mahogany cowboy boots, the toes worn and scuffed, caught my attention as I tried to envision their owner. Shoes of an apparently successful businessman sat alongside a pair evidently belonging to a humble farmer. Some of the shoes bore name-brand labels that were easy to read; others had no label at all.

Where had those shoes traveled? What journeys had brought them to rest at the temple doors for a few hours? I felt there was so much to learn, but with responsibilities waiting inside, I left the sermon of the shoes for a time.

As matron of the temple, I yearned to know all that I could as quickly as possible. I came to understand that my knowledge would grow line upon line, and that my first task was to become acquainted with the good people with whom we would be serving. I soon discovered that I had a desire not just to know the names of these people but also to know *them*, hoping we could become dear friends rather than just co-workers.

After becoming acquainted with a brother or sister in the temple, I often realized with regret that if I had met that person in another setting—the marketplace, the post office, or even at church—I may not have recognized the possibility of a close and valued friendship. Could a difference in age or interests, the color or style of her dress, her social status, or even her shoes possibly have interfered with this almost instant and deep friendship that I experienced in the temple?

I believe the first layer of the "sermon in their shoes" was coming into focus. I wanted to go back and report, "I think I am beginning to get it."

Christian philosopher C. S. Lewis addresses in his writing this divine relationship between people: "It is a serious thing to live in a society of possible gods and goddesses, to remember that the dullest and most uninteresting person you talk to may one day be a creature which . . . you would be strongly tempted to worship, or else a horror and a corruption such as you now meet, if at all, only in a nightmare. All day long we are, in some degree, helping each other to one or other of these destinations. It is in the light of these overwhelming possibilities, it is with the awe and the circumspection proper to them, that we should conduct all our dealings with one another, all friendships, all loves, all play, all politics. There are no *ordinary* people. You have never talked to a mere mortal" (*The Joyful Christian* [New York: Macmillan, 1977], 197).

Once inside the temple, that truth is more clear. We see no ordinary people but rather potential gods and goddesses.

Again I returned to the shoe racks at the entrance

to the temple. Looking at the shoes, I had a spiritual awakening. It was not the shoes that I was to focus on. I shouldn't study the shoes and then go inside and try to play a matching game of who owned which pair. It didn't matter. Symbolically, when faithful Saints step out of their shoes and step into the temple, they are leaving the world behind. Inside the temple there is nothing of the world to separate us, classify us, or elevate one above another. The ultimate blessings of the temple are promised to everyone, regardless of the factors that we sometimes see as indicators of our worth: intellect, social status, position, title, or even number of children or grandchildren.

In the temple we join with faithful Latter-day Saints on our journey home, walking with faith in every footstep, learning truths we need to know to be received by our Heavenly Father. The Lord looketh on the heart, not the shoes, and so must we. In the temple there is a remarkable spirit of love, acceptance, and concern for one another. Every soul is of equal worth—regardless of the condition of the person's shoes out on the rack. Deep and precious friendships are formed that cross every culture, nationality, and age. I have come to believe that the sermon of the shoes was intended only as a symbol by which we might see past the shoes and see our brothers and sisters as they really are. When we cast our eyes on the heart and the soul of another, we begin to understand the worth of that soul and the promised blessings of the temple, for all who come remove their shoes, even as Moses, and feel the reality of being on holy ground in the House of the Lord.

3

HOW FAR DO YOU LIVE FROM THE TEMPLE?

I stood in the doorway of the chapel inside the temple, quietly greeting brothers and sisters dressed in white as they came in to wait for the next session to begin. This was not an infrequent experience for me, but this time something was different. I was drawn by the music that filled the room, creating a special feeling of reverence. Instead of leaving after a quick check that all was in order, I took a seat at the far side where I could sit quietly and listen. The room was filled with a spirit of worship. No one was whispering. The familiar strains of "Nearer, My God, to Thee" were being played with such feeling that the music sounded like a testimony coming from the heart of the organist.

After the chapel had emptied, I was eager to speak with the organist, Diane Miller, and express gratitude for her wonderful service. I had first met Sister Miller ten years previously, when my husband and I were serving in the Canada Vancouver Mission. She and her husband and three children lived in Terrace, in the far northern part of British Columbia. On our first of many visits to Terrace, we became acquainted with the Miller family. They were the backbone of the small branch of the Church there. Sister Miller was serving as district Young Women president, branch Young Women president, branch organist, and later as teacher of home-study seminary and the teenage Sunday School class. The load was heavy, the winter nights were long, the roads in the winter were treacherous, and distant travel was required to go anywhere. The dedication of the Miller family was never in question, I thought with a smile as I watched Sister Miller play.

When those attending the session had left the chapel, I walked over to the organ and slid onto the bench beside Sister Miller. I waited while she finished playing "More Holiness Give Me," hearing in my mind the words:

> *More fit for the kingdom,*
> *More used would I be,*
> *More blessed and holy—*
> *More, Savior, like thee.*
>
> —HYMNS, NO. 131

The notes on the last line were sustained, as if Sister Miller was reluctant to bring her assignment for the day to a close. Leaning back from the organ, with her short arms stretched forward, she raised her hands from the keys in benediction.

I spoke in quiet tones, not wanting to break the spirit in the room. "Diane, you play with such feeling," I said. "Tell me about your calling to play the organ in the temple."

"I love music," she began. "For me, music is my way of expressing my love for the Lord. I have a hard time putting my thoughts and feelings into words. I play the hymns, think of the words in my mind, and feel such peace. I just love to be here. It is something I have dreamed of forever."

Noticing that her small hands were swollen and that she seemed to struggle to reach the keys, I asked, "How is your health?"

Joyfully she responded with a smile, "Good enough to be here!" Then she added, almost incidentally, "I have lupus, and also two kinds of arthritis, one of which is in the muscles and tendons around the joints. My hands stiffen and swell, but I have missed my assignment only once since I started ten months ago, and that was to attend my niece's wedding in the Seattle Temple."

"Where do you live now?" I asked.

She told me that she and her family lived in Arrdrie, north of Calgary. "We had to leave Terrace to find work," she explained. "We lived on Church welfare for a few months. My husband left for Alberta to find employment, and we wanted to be closer to the temple. Our prayer was answered. He got a job in the north of Calgary. I put our house up for sale in a depressed market and sold it in six days. The Lord has blessed us. My two girls and I packed up the van and headed for Alberta. We were reunited as a family just in time for Christmas." Tears of gratitude were streaming down her face. "My husband had work, and we had rented a three-bedroom town house. Daniel, our son, had left on his mission to Halifax, so he was not with us at the time. Later my husband's sister and her husband had some difficulties, so we said, 'Please come and live with us,' and we're getting along just fine."

I knew that Arrdrie was about a three-hour drive from the temple in good weather, and longer in the winter storms. I asked how she managed that.

"I leave about 5:15 in the morning," she explained.

"That would mean you drive three hours in the dark in the wintertime, right?"

She smiled. "There isn't much traffic at that time of day. I've learned to drive on icy roads, and I don't get frightened."

I tried to imagine the challenges of driving, usually alone; getting sleepy (since she said she could hardly sleep the night before for fear of missing her alarm); health problems; or simply the discomfort of sitting on the hard bench in front of the organ for three hours with only a brief break between sessions. I asked, "What is the hardest part about this calling, coming to the temple every other week to play the organ?"

Her response was quick: "There is really only one problem. Financially it has been very difficult. It costs about fifty dollars each round trip, and that is hard for us, but my husband is so supportive. He knows how much I love music and how much it means to me to be called to play the organ in the temple. There is so little I can do because of my health. If I waited until we could afford it, I might not have the health to do it." She stretched out her swollen fingers and then, being short, she struggled to lift herself down from the bench she was sitting on. Again she expressed gratitude. "I am so grateful for this calling because with my health there are so few other things I can do. It is such a blessing to live so close to a temple."

"*Close* to the temple?" I questioned.

"Yes," she said in a tone of gratitude. "When we lived in Terrace, whether we went to the Seattle Temple or the Cardston Temple, it was about 1,070 miles one way." Then she emphasized, "This is close; it's really not that far."

Having finished her time for playing the organ that day, Diane Miller picked up her cane and made her way to the area where she would prepare to serve as a proxy for one of her family members. "I have so many family names! I am anxious to do their temple work as fast as I can," she explained. "I joined the Church when I was thirteen years old. My best friends were Latter-day Saints, and one day I asked if I could go to church with them. The Sunday I went, I was so surprised to see my brother there. He was secretly meeting with the missionaries and taking the discussions. When my parents found out, they said we could have the missionaries come to our home. My brother was baptized. My parents never joined the Church, and they insisted that a thirteen-year-old wasn't old enough to know her own mind. I persisted until they gave permission, and

I have been an active member ever since. I have a lot of work to do," she said. And off she went to do it.

"How far do I live from the temple?" It is an interesting question to ponder, particularly when we think about it not in terms of hours or miles or kilometers but rather in terms of readiness or attitude or preparation. Some people whose houses are within blocks of the temple may be living further away from its blessings than my friends in Terrace, and it may take them longer to get there.

How far do you live from a temple? How long does it take to get there? Maybe it isn't a question of distance but of priorities. May we all examine our lives more closely and make whatever effort is required to draw our hearts closer to the temple and the promised blessings.

4

REMEMBER

I wonder why it is that the sense of smell can return a total experience to the consciousness even better, I think, than sight or sound. For instance, the faint, sweet smell of lilac dusting powder returns me to my grandmother's side with an emotion not recalled for years. I see my Grandma Greene, who lived in our home during my childhood, standing at the ironing board and wearing her black slippers with little holes cut on the outer edges near the big toe to "let her bunions out." I see her long, gray hair in a neat bob, "easy to care for," she insisted. Over the old ironing board, which dropped down from the wall in the kitchen, she stood for hours ironing her temple clothes—freshly washed after each trip to the temple. A small whiff of lilac perfume, in any situation, and it seems my grandmother is not far away.

Next to smell, as a magical vehicle to wipe away time and distance, I would vote for music. The other day the tune "Near You," popular in the Big Band era, found its way through the airwaves and into our living room. In an instant I was transported back in time. I could see the popular band behind their bandstands with their names written in large script across the front, *The Blue Bombers*. I remember the boy I was waltzing with and the one I wished I had been waltzing with that evening. I even remember what I wore: a dirndl skirt that flared out when I swung under my partner's arm with the last measure of music floating on the evening breeze beyond the pavilion.

Memories can also be summoned by more tangible things. A tiny wildflower I picked years ago from an open field in Karonita, New Zealand, remains tucked in my scriptures to this day. It brings back all the memories associated with the faith of those Maori people whom I came to love. A small rock from the shore of the Sea of Galilee returns to the memory glorious experiences to be relived again and again in remarkable detail.

And tucked away in my top dresser drawer is a small pile of white handkerchiefs. When I open that drawer and catch a glimpse of this collection, I am transported for a magical moment to other times and places. One handkerchief restores to my mind the incredible feeling of being in attendance at the dedication of the Las Vegas Temple. Words are inadequate to convey the scope of that experience, which reached beyond my previous awareness. Another handkerchief brings to mind in great detail the dedication of the Toronto Temple and the feeling of grandeur associated with blessings made available only in the House of the Lord. Another handkerchief, looking a bit used with touches of makeup and signs of joyous tears, brings back the memories of the rededication of the Cardston Alberta Temple. History records that my Grandfather Greene with his team of horses broke the sod when construction was begun on the original building in 1913.

I pick up another handkerchief and, although I was not present except through the blessing of satellite transmission, it recalls memories of the dedication of the Palmyra Temple. Another handkerchief traveled in my pocket to the dedication of the great Conference Center in Salt Lake City, and one more is a reminder of the dedication of the historic Winter Quarters Temple and the tremendous sacrifice of the early Saints.

More than smell, more than music, more than objects, it is the Spirit that reawakens again and again the deep, inner feelings associated with such important events. In each case, I hear in my mind again the prophet's voice in a prayer of dedication. Being present to hear the prophet in prayer to the Lord surely thins the veil.

At the dedication of the Conference Center, President Gordon B. Hinckley explained, "Now, my brothers and sisters, in a moment I shall offer the dedicatory prayer, in which all of you are invited to join. Immediately at the close of the dedicatory prayer, we invite each one of you who may wish to participate to stand and join with us in the Hosanna Shout. This sacred salute to the Father and the Son is given at the dedication of each of the temples. It has also been given on a few occasions of historic importance, such as the laying of the capstone on the Salt Lake Temple and the celebration of the centennial of the Church in the 1930 general conference.

"We feel it is appropriate to give the shout here, as we dedicate this great building, the likes of which we may never undertake again. . . . I will now demonstrate the shout. Each one takes a clean white handkerchief, holding it by one corner, and waves it while saying in unison, 'Hosanna, Hosanna, Hosanna to God and the Lamb,' repeated three times, followed by

'Amen, Amen, and Amen'" (*Ensign*, November 2000, 69–70).

"The Hosanna Shout," according to the *Encyclopedia of Mormonism*, "is whole-souled, given to the full limit of one's strength. . . . The Hosanna Shout memorializes the pre-earthly Council in Heaven, as 'when . . . all the sons of God shouted for joy' (Job 38:7). It also recalls the hosannas and the waving of palm branches accorded the Messiah as he entered Jerusalem. And hosannas welcomed him as he appeared to the Nephites. President Lorenzo Snow taught that this shout will herald in the Messiah when he comes in the glory of the Father (cf. 1 Thes. 4:16)" (Daniel H. Ludlow, ed., *Encyclopedia of Mormonism* [New York: Macmillan, 1992], 2:659).

It is one thing to read about such an event, but it is quite another to participate in an emotional experience that encompasses the whole being. Under a white cloud of 21,000 people waving white handkerchiefs and in unison repeating the words as directed, I felt my soul stirred and my mind expanded in ways never to be forgotten.

Looking upon a small pile of white handkerchiefs tucked away in my drawer, I see a great white cloud overhead that transports me back—or maybe forward—

in time and space. I can hear "The Hosanna Anthem" sung by the choir, with the congregation joining in singing "The Spirit of God," and it seems the armies of heaven join in the chorus:

> *The Spirit of God like a fire is burning!*
> *The latter-day glory begins to come forth;*
> *The visions and blessings of old are returning,*
> *And angels are coming to visit the earth.*
>
> *We'll sing and we'll shout with the armies of heaven,*
> *Hosanna, hosanna to God and the Lamb!*
> *Let glory to them in the highest be given,*
> *Henceforth and forever, Amen and amen!*
>
> —HYMNS, NO. 2

There are, no doubt, many white handkerchiefs tucked away in drawers with precious memories related to more than 100 temple dedications. Can we possibly remember the occasion of a temple dedication without a deep sense of rededication in our own lives to the very purpose of the important work to be accomplished within the walls of these temples? How grateful I am to have participated in several such events, and to be reminded, each time I see my own small pile of handkerchiefs, of the great hosts of heaven I hope one day to join in shouting hosannas to my King!

5

HOOKED ON
SPIRITUAL AEROBICS

It is true that some things become habit form-
ing. Once you get started, you just don't want to quit.
But I'm thinking of an instance when this feeling
comes not like an enslaving addiction but rather as a
feeling of exhilaration that generates newfound energy.
Those who have become hooked are the first to
acknowledge their fever and want to spread their mal-
ady wherever and whenever possible.

Considering those who seem most susceptible to
this condition, I would have confidently defended the
probability that until at least middle age, there is little
risk of contracting it. Then, one day, I found on my
desk in the matron's office of the temple a two-page
letter addressed to me. It was not in an envelope, nor
was it folded; rather, it was handwritten in ink on
parchment-type pages and rolled like an ancient scroll
around sticks both top and bottom. Some irregularity
in the letters, a few scribbled-out words, and one or

two spelling errors suggested the labor of someone rather young. I immediately unrolled this curious document and began reading:

"Dear Sister Kapp,

"About 2 years ago a man named Jim Marsh took the missionary discussions in our home. Jim was baptized on the 15th of May 1999. He was excited, and his greatest desire was to be sealed to his wife, who had died 5 years earlier of cancer. He died on March 24, 2000, only 2 months before the sealing would take place."

An account of this kind was not unfamiliar to me, and although such a story always holds interest, I sensed something unusual about this bit of history. The letter continued:

"Before Brother Marsh died, he had my mother promise to do his family history. My mother did promise, and three months later received a book containing the start of Brother Marsh's family history. Not knowing where to begin, my mom leafed through the book and found a name belonging to Mrs. Joyce Tabler. On impulse my mom phoned her and found that she was researching Jim's line, and would gladly share any information that she had. Mrs. Tabler sent us a disk with not only Jim's line but her husband's line also. Although she was not a member of the Church, she wanted her husband's Tabler line done too. Brother Kevin Louder copied the disk, and Mom started to fill in the blanks. This is how I got involved. My mom asked me to go with her to the Family History Library to help her. I started. I could not stop. Soon I was inviting my friend Kendall Stockdale to come with me. I got her hooked, and together we found a bundle of names. *Hooked* is the right expression here, and finding a 'bundle of names' is a sure sign of being on the verge of becoming hooked for life."

She explained the process: "In a little while we fell into a routine. We couldn't stop. As soon as we finished writing down information on a child, we would look some more and find another. I turned 12 on May 1st, and I have been looking forward to doing baptisms for the dead for a long time. I am excited to do the work in the temple that I did in the Family History Library.

"Thank you for the opportunity to write this letter.

"Yours truly,

"Ashley Toone

"P.S. Doing baptisms is a much greater reward than money."

I love to walk past the great baptismal font in the temple and see the youth dressed in their white jump-suits, young men and young women who choose to set aside other things, step out of the world for a time, and wait their turn to perform these sacred ordi-nances. I stand quietly, trying to control my emotions, as I hear the sound of water—splash, splash, down and up, again and again—knowing that each time another noble soul has been released from spirit prison by a youth acting as one of the saviors on mount Zion.

Alongside the sacred records recorded on parch-ment in another time and place, would not the hand-written record of twelve-year-old Ashley be considered one of the great testimonies of our time? Her words show that this is indeed the time spoken of by the Prophet Malachi: "Behold, I will send you Elijah the prophet before the coming of the great and dreadful day of the Lord: And he shall turn the heart of the fathers to the children, and the heart of the children to their fathers, lest I come and smite the earth with a curse" (Malachi 4:5–6).

As I read that scripture, I see in my mind's eye one twelve-year-old girl hooked on this great work of redemption for the dead, and others like her who come to the temple to do for those who have gone before what they cannot do for themselves. My heart rejoices as I recognize the turning of the hearts of the children to their fathers and the fulfillment of prophecy in the temples of the Lord.

6

A FEAR
AND A PRAYER

$\mathscr{I}$ had been to Calgary two or maybe three times in my life, but never had I been aware of the cemetery near the entrance to the city. This time, as I sat in the backseat of the car nursing a terrible headache, I noticed as we passed by the graveyard endless headstones as far as I could see. My mind raced through countless possibilities and tremendous fears. I was afraid I was going to die.

I was fifteen years old. My mother and father were miles from home, and my grandmother was staying with me. While my parents were away, I had developed a serious ear infection. The local doctor explained to my anxious grandmother that my condition was serious and would require immediate surgery. I would need to be taken to a hospital in Calgary, a distance of about three hours from my home. An aunt and uncle sharing in the concern were quite willing to set aside what they were doing and make the rush trip to the hospital.

Arrangements had been made by our doctor for my care immediately upon my arrival at the hospital. All this unexpected concern for my welfare only added to my fear. I became focused on one concern. Yes, I realized I might not live—an idea reinforced by the doctor's sense of urgency for me to get to Calgary and the immediate proximity of the cemetery we had driven by—but that was not my main worry. My main concern was for my mom and dad. Could they be reached? I knew they would come home as soon as word of my condition reached them. But it had been years since they had enjoyed even a few days of vacation, and they were traveling somewhere in California with friends on a long-anticipated trip. The surgery would need to take place in their absence. In my young mind, my major concern was that of spoiling their holiday. How would they feel if they returned from a vacation to face my funeral? I remember hoping that they wouldn't feel too guilty for being away when I needed them. I wanted them to know I did not blame them; I didn't want them to feel sad.

All this happened before the modern miracle of today's medicines and surgical procedures, so following the surgery I lay in a hospital bed, and my entire head, except for my face, was heavily bandaged. Even so, I overheard one of the doctors telling the nurse that the infection in my left ear had been so severe that I would possibly lose my equilibrium and my hearing. I wasn't even sure what *equilibrium* meant, but I feared the thought of being deaf.

My family got hold of my parents in Long Beach, California. They drove all day and all night, not stopping at home but driving the additional three hours to the hospital in Calgary, arriving early on the morning following the surgery. They looked tired and worried as they leaned over my bed, held my hands, and talked to me, and I could feel their anxiety and their love. The surgery was behind me, but the healing process was of major concern, according to the doctor.

There in that hospital room, my father placed his hands upon my shaven head, which was mostly wrapped in bandages, and gave me a blessing. A wonderful feeling of peace came over me.

In a tone that assured me all would be well, my mother explained to me that she would have my name placed on the prayer roll in the Cardston Alberta Temple, not far from our home. It was the first time I realized that a person could have his or her name placed on a prayer roll in the temple. The fear left me. Somehow the idea of having my name written in the temple, where I would be prayed for, was something I had never known was possible. I felt an almost overwhelming feeling of importance and hoped I was good enough to have my name written in the temple.

Within weeks I could walk steadily, and my hearing was back to normal. Instead of losing my hearing in my left ear, it has remained stronger than in my right. Even today I always put the telephone to my left ear because my hearing is better in that ear.

Since that frightening experience years ago, I have become acquainted with another kind of hearing, not with my ears but rather in my mind and my heart. Through that traumatic experience in my youth, I have a better understanding of how I was saved from what I feared might be a premature funeral.

President Gordon B. Hinckley's words explain, "Believe in prayer. There is nothing like it. When all is said and done there is no power on earth like the power of prayer" (*Church News*, January 29, 2000).

Today, I often pause as I observe those who stop by a small table just inside the temple to place on the prayer roll the name of a loved one or friend in need of a special blessing. I wonder what my mother, who passed away years ago, would think if she knew I was now watching over the prayer roll and other areas in this very temple where she placed my name all those years ago. I believe she knows.

FOR TIME
AND ALL ETERNITY

*W*orld War II had ended. Many lives had been lost in the cause of freedom. Families were being reunited. Having served their country, some young men had returned home only to set aside their future plans once again in response to the call to serve the Lord on a mission.

One such young man had just returned from the Navy, having spent sixteen months at sea on an attack troop transport, and he was anxious for a change. When asked by a General Authority where he might like to serve his mission, he responded quickly, "Anywhere, but preferably not Canada. I hate the cold." His request was acknowledged, and he waited for his call.

One eventful day a letter arrived. In bold type were the words *Western Canadian Mission*. With little preparation, the new missionary left his widowed mother and boarded the train to Edmonton, in the northern part of the province of Alberta. It was February, the dead of winter. The mission president, a Canadian himself and acquainted with severe temperatures, had established a mission-wide policy: When the temperature dropped lower than forty degrees below zero, permission was given to stop tracting and remain indoors. For days the temperature registered forty-below, but only once or twice did it take even a dip beneath that. Freezing February dragged into March, then cold and windy April and May. It was a bleak launching for this young man's mission.

Come July, the reward for his dedication surpassed anything he had imagined. All the missionaries from the provinces of Saskatchewan on the east to Alberta and British Columbia on the west were instructed to travel by bus or train and meet together at the historic Cardston Alberta Temple in a mission-wide conference.

Cardston, being a town of only about 2,500, provided minimal accommodations for the influx of people. The missionaries were billeted out to the members' homes for one or two nights. Six elders were taken to a small town twenty miles away, where two of them stayed in the bishop's home. One was the young man from the Navy, and of that event he recorded a brief journal entry in passing: "I met the bishop's daughter and she is cute and fun but kind of young."

President Edward J. Wood, the president of the Cardston Temple, had served thirty-nine years as stake president and twenty-five years as temple president concurrently. He was known as a spiritual giant, with many faith-promoting manifestations and testimonies of miracles that had occurred in the temple. Meeting the president of the Cardston Temple and being taught by him within its walls about the eternal nature of things eradicated any feeling of sacrifice this missionary had endured. This experience would leave a deep and abiding impression in his life.

Years later he would remember the impact of the words he read on a bronze plaque at the entrance of the temple. The early apostle Orson F. Whitney, with his inspirational and poetic spirit, composed for the dedication of this temple in 1923 a message that remains today. These words convey to visitors the very essence of the temple:

> *Hearts must be pure to come within these walls,*
> *Where spreads a feast unknown to festive halls.*
> *Freely partake, for freely God hath given,*
> *And taste the holy joys that tell of heaven.*
> *Here learn of him who triumphed o'er the grave,*

> *And unto men the keys, the Kingdom, gave;*
> *Joined here by powers that past and present bind*
> *The living and the dead perfection find.*

In the temple President Wood spoke of the celestial kingdom and increased the missionaries' understanding: "In the celestial glory there are three heavens or degrees; and in order to obtain the highest, a man must enter into this order of the priesthood [meaning the new and everlasting covenant of marriage]; and if he does not, he cannot obtain it" (D&C 131:1–3). This missionary gained a deeper understanding of the blessings associated with the ordinances and covenants of the temple and the eternal nature of families. As he taught people the importance of baptism, the first step toward those glorious blessings, these lessons would remain in his mind and sustain him in the coming months.

Following his mission, with the help of the GI Bill, a government allowance for men who had served their country, he would pursue his education. While at school he once again met the bishop's daughter and found her to be still "cute and fun but kind of young."

A friendship developed. The following summer, no longer a missionary, the young man returned to the bishop's home as a welcomed guest. The evening after his arrival, he and the bishop's daughter sat on the hill near the Prince of Wales Hotel at Waterton National Park, overlooking Waterton Lakes in the majestic Canadian Rockies. They talked for a long time. There was a full moon that night, with a few scattered clouds. The young man made the observation that if they watched long enough, the moon would go behind the cloud, but that if they continued watching, in time the full moon would come out again. "That's how life is," he explained. Then he made an offer to the young woman from a small country village. Although the offer was very attractive, the idea of giving up her maiden name, citizenship, *and horse* caused a momentary delay in her response. But on the early morning of June 28, 1950, the former missionary and the bishop's daughter returned to the Cardston Temple, there to be sealed for time and all eternity.

Of this grand blessing concerning the eternal family organization, as it was first revealed to and taught by the Prophet Joseph Smith, Parley P. Pratt recorded, "It was from him that I learned that the wife of my bosom might be secured to me for time and all eternity; and that the refined sympathies and affections which endeared us to each other emanated from the fountain of divine eternal love. It was from him that I learned that we might cultivate these affections, and grow and increase in the same to all eternity; while the result of our endless union would be an offspring as numerous as the stars of heaven, or the sands of the sea shore" (*Autobiography of Parley P. Pratt* [Salt Lake City: Deseret Book, 1985], 260).

The morning following their sealing, the young couple, now a family, was stepping into their future together with the promise of a rich inheritance through obedience—"and [they] shall inherit thrones, kingdoms, principalities, and powers, dominions, all heights and depths" (D&C 132:19)—a grand promise for a couple starting out with so little.

In this marriage, throughout the years, there were blessings unmeasured, beyond anything that might ever have been expected. There were also some unfulfilled expectations. The couple learned from personal experience the importance of the words of the Savior: "My people must be tried in all things, that they may be prepared to receive the glory that I have for them, even the glory of Zion" (D&C 136:31).

Throughout the years they returned to temples in other locations. In good times and in hard times they received answers to prayers. And when an earnest request for a blessing was delayed, there was, in time, a calming peace found in the temple.

Then, in September 2000, fifty years since that day of sealing in the Cardston Alberta Temple, a call came from the office of the First Presidency of the Church. The prophet asked, "Heber, how are you?" and the once-young Western Canadian missionary responded, "Just fine, except for a few aches and pains of old age." The ninety-year-old prophet chuckled in response, "Oh, you're only a kid," and then he issued a call to the couple to serve as the president and matron of the Cardston Alberta Temple. The wife responded with excitement at the thought of returning home, but then she was struck by a sudden realization: "But I remember the temple presidents as being old men!" With words used in years past, now slightly modified, the husband repeated, "The bishop's daughter is still cute and fun but *not* so young."

The first day in our calling at the Cardston Temple, we paused at the bronze plaque and read once again with a deeper understanding and appreciation the promise, "Joined here by powers that past and present bind/The living and the dead perfection find." We better understand now the feelings expressed by Parley P. Pratt: "Joseph Smith, had barely touched a single key;

had merely lifted a corner of the veil and given me a single glance into eternity" (*Autobiography of Parley P. Pratt,* 260).

After more than fifty years of striving to keep the covenants we made with each other and the Lord, in the evenings as we walk (or perhaps a more accurate word might be *shuffle*) around the temple and look up at the night sky, regardless of the weather, from our perspective it appears that there is a full moon with no clouds. We feel the blessings of promises made and promises to keep for time and all eternity.

8

THE SISTERS
AT BADGER VALLEY

*B*adger Valley might rightly be referred to as a "righteous hangout." About a thirty-minute drive from the Cardston Temple, partly on a gravel road, stands a large, rustic, one-story building with open fields on all sides. The view to the west is framed in the distance by the majestic Rocky Mountains, with Old Chief Mountain in its position of prominence. Like a giant sentinel it stands, keeping protective watch over all who gather here for fun, friendship, and the building of memories. To the north stretches the vast Canadian prairie with tall grass sprinkled with wild flowers. Although I am not aware of anyone ever having seen a badger at Badger Valley, it is not uncommon to see deer, elk, rabbits, and occasionally a moose or an antelope. A feeling of intruding into territory that has already been claimed invites a sense of reverence for this pristine area.

Inside the Badger Valley building, as it is called, are

large rooms for gathering, smaller rooms for overnight accommodations, and a kitchen. However, my experience at Badger Valley verifies that time spent in friendship far outweighs the desire for food requiring lengthy preparation. Dress is casual, appropriate for the setting. It is a place where time stands still and quiet conversation often continues late into the night.

Having been invited on several occasions to meet with young women in this setting, I was familiar with the area and full of anticipation as I prepared to meet there with a group of Relief Society sisters. The plan explained to me by the president of the Relief Society was to provide an evening of fast food, fun, friendship, and goodwill, culminating with a fireside in preparation for their commitment to attend the temple the following morning.

When I arrived at the appointed hour, any differences in marital status, interests, age, or other distinctions that might interfere with the feeling of closeness had faded away. The sisters were drawn together beside a large fireplace. The evening temperature was cool, and the fire provided welcome warmth, adding to the atmosphere created by twenty-five good women sitting together side by side in a large circle, chatting and caring for one another in this remote area. I learned during the evening of severe challenges some of the sisters carried: disappointments, unfulfilled expectations, prayers not yet answered, worries, and some anxieties. Yet with it all came a spirit of love, peace, unity, faith, and hope.

One sister who had appeared thoughtful during the fireside posed a question that focused everyone's attention, perhaps in anticipation of the following morning. "How do you learn in the temple?" she asked.

"Just go there," came a quick, seemingly obvious response. But this was not enough.

"No," she said. "I do go, but I'm not sure I get it." Immediately this sincere inquiry invited the attention of each sister in the circle. How do you *learn* in the temple?

One of the younger sisters, who later was identified to me as a seminary teacher, opened her scriptures, a handbook for such inquiry. "Turn to the book of Mosiah," she directed. "This is where King Benjamin is addressing his people who have come up to the temple to be taught. I think there is a pattern here for us." She stood before the group and read, "'*Hearken unto me*, and *open your ears* that ye may *hear*, and *your hearts* that ye may *understand*, and your minds that the mysteries of God may be unfolded to your view'"

[Mosiah 2:9; emphasis added]. "The Holy Ghost speaks to our minds and our hearts," she explained, turning to Doctrine and Covenants 8:2: "'Yea, behold, I will tell you in your mind and in your heart, by the Holy Ghost, which shall come upon you and which shall dwell in your heart.'"

Another sister, anxious to ease any concerns, said, "I don't think we are expected to 'get it all' in the first or even the hundredth time, but I think there is a pattern that helps us be better prepared to learn each time we return to the temple." With her scriptures open she continued, "Listen to the words of the Savior speaking to the multitude when he visited the American continent. He had been teaching the people important lessons. They did not want him to leave. He continued to teach them." Lowering her voice, she read, "'I perceive that ye are weak, that ye cannot understand all my words which I am commanded of the Father to speak unto you at this time.'"

"Now, here is the pattern," she explained. "'Therefore, go ye unto your homes, and *ponder* upon the things which I have said, and *ask* of the Father, in my name, that ye may *understand*, and *prepare your minds* for the morrow, and I *come unto you again*' [3 Nephi 17:2–3; emphasis added]. When I go home from the temple with questions, I try to ponder and ask and pray, and I'm more ready and anxious to be taught each time I go."

After we had spent some time listening to and learning from each other in an open, trusting exchange, one sister summed it up by repeating the earlier response that at first had seemed a bit flippant. "I think I've got it," she said. "Just go there—" Then she added, "hungering for knowledge."

The words of Elder L. Lionel Kendrick provide understanding of the process for learning through temple attendance. He explains, "The Spirit of the Holy Ghost is the teacher in the temple. He teaches principles of eternal significance. It is during these instructions that we see the relationship between the earthly and the eternal. We must remember that the Spirit teaches only those who are teachable. If we enter the temple seeking added light and knowledge, we can learn and understand something new during the temple experience. The Savior promised: 'That which is of God is light; and he that . . . continueth in God, receiveth more light; and that light groweth brighter and brighter until the perfect day' (D&C 50:24)" (*Ensign*, May 2001, 79).

The crackling fire had died down, and the soft

lights in the cabin cast a glow over the gathering. Some sisters wrapped themselves in blankets as if to retain the warmth of the evening—not necessarily the heat from the fire. The occasion had been rich with insights, shared testimonies, and lessons taught by the Spirit. The earnest supplication of the opening prayer had been realized. Time had come to retire.

On Saturday morning, most of the sisters who had gathered at Badger Valley the night before were in the temple for the first session, sitting side by side, dressed in white, anticipating what they would learn through personal revelation. Upon leaving the temple, their leader expressed her feelings, "It was more than we could have hoped for." A promise that one sister shared from her patriarchal blessing resounded in a promise for all who attend the temple worthily: "Every time you go to the temple you will receive spiritual blessings and a better understanding of the gospel of Jesus Christ."

9

ANOTHER RESCUE

*S*he looked like an angel.

A little girl in a heavy white cotton jumpsuit, bursting with anticipation and excitement, stood near the stairs leading up to the baptismal font in the Cardston Alberta Temple. She had long dark hair and big brown eyes and a complexion that appeared to have been kissed by the sun. She stood *anxiously* waiting her turn.

The large font in the center of the room, surrounded on all sides by walls of marble twenty feet high, rests on the back and shoulders of twelve large, beautifully sculpted oxen. The oxen stand in a circle with heads facing outward and heavy horns reaching upward, with tall, decorative grass and a few flowers between each, creating an imposing sight. In the grandeur of this majestic setting, little Jetta appeared so small, so young, so pure and innocent that I felt compelled to ask if she was really "of age" to perform the sacred ordinance of baptisms for the dead.

"How old is she?" I asked her mother, who was standing nearby.

"She turned twelve a few days ago, and this is her first time at the temple," her mother explained. Then she drew my attention to her two dark-haired sons, Jetta's older brothers, who were sharing in this important occasion. It was apparent that her brothers were eager to be identified with their sister. This was obviously a special family activity, a celebration, an event that had been in the planning for some time, maybe years.

The children's devoted mother shepherded her little flock as each child eagerly waited his or her turn to climb the five steps to the top of the font. There each one paused before stepping down into the warm water where the sacred ordinance of baptism would be performed. This is what young Jetta had requested in celebration of her twelfth birthday. Did Jetta know that this would be a celebration not only for her and her family but also for other faithful Saints on the other side of the veil? Did she know that this event recorded on earth would also be recorded in heaven?

I'm sure Jetta's family celebrated her birthday as a

happy remembrance of the day she was born. It seems fitting that, through her desire to perform the ordinance of baptism for someone who could not perform it for herself, Jetta was providing an opportunity and blessing for that person to be "born again."

Those who die without the blessing of baptism must wait until someone comes to their rescue and stands in their behalf, acting as proxy for them. Someone must do for them what they cannot do for themselves.

This notion of rescue is captured in the story of the Martin and Willie handcart companies, sometimes referred to by historians as *the rescue*. History records that it was late in the season when a group of faithful Saints pushing handcarts left Iowa City headed for the Salt Lake Valley. They had gotten as far as Wyoming when freezing temperatures and lack of provisions stopped them in their tracks. The handcart companies were utterly helpless. Had Brigham Young not sent rescuers out with blankets and food, they all would have died, like ten-year-old Bodil Mortensen: "Exhausted and weak, the intrepid young Danish girl closed her eyes for the last time that day. Her frozen little body was later found by company members: her spirit was now in a safe, warm place" (Susan Arrington Madsen,

The Second Rescue [Salt Lake City: Deseret Book, 1998], 4).

On October 22, 2001, 144 years from the very day of their rescue, while participating in a seminar of newly called temple presidents and their wives, President Gordon B. Hinckley reviewed with us the condition of these Saints in the Martin and Willie handcart companies. He spoke of their desperate plight, explaining that they had gone as far as they possibly could. With some emotion, President Hinckley said: "These people gave everything they had." Then he explained that this is the situation millions are in today—millions of people on the other side of the veil who have no means to help themselves. "They are waiting on us," he said. "We are the rescue party."

"On August 14, 1991, in one of those sacred houses of the Lord, the name of the little Danish girl, Bodil Mortensen, was spoken again, reverently and authoritatively. On that day Sarah Lorimer, age fifteen, entered the Ogden Temple in Utah and was baptized for and in behalf of Bodil" (Madsen, *Second Rescue*, 5).

It wasn't a bad winter day when Jetta and her brothers and mother came to the temple to perform sacred temple ordinances for those waiting. They did not face a severe blizzard like those who went to rescue the Willie and Martin handcart companies. But make no mistake, it was a rescue indeed.

Twelve-year-old Jetta served as proxy and came to the rescue, opening the door for a sister somewhere, maybe even a ten-year-old girl like the little Danish girl. It is likely that this individual will one day be her true and dear friend. The Prophet Joseph Smith taught that in the resurrection those whose temple work had been done by proxy would fall at the feet of those who had done their work, kiss their feet, embrace their knees, and manifest the most exquisite gratitude (see Truman Madsen, *Joseph Smith the Prophet* [Salt Lake City: Bookcraft, 1989], 99). The celebration of young Jetta's birthday would provide occasion for a new friend to be released from spirit prison.

As I walk through the temple many times a day, past the wide stairway leading to the baptismal font, sometimes all is quiet. The water in the font is still, and no one is around. At other times I hear the sound of glorious events taking place.

Young Jetta had an unusual birthday wish. She wanted to give a gift of eternal value to someone she didn't even know. Every time I hear the splash of water in the baptismal font of the temple, I know that someone is making that desire a reality, giving another the opportunity to be born again through the waters of baptism. What happier birthday could there be?

10

AN INFALLIBLE GUIDE

*O*nce when I was in Texas on an assignment, I was invited to visit the Jake Garn Mission Simulator and Training Facility in Houston. It is the prime facility for training flight crews in all their activities in the space shuttle program. I was given the incredible opportunity to be commander of the ship during a simulated trip into space.

Climbing two flights of stairs, I entered the door of this remarkable spacecraft and was strapped into the command seat. My heart began to pound, it all seemed so real. It was explained to me that I would be guiding the ship through space. I had no former experience. I would have preferred being a passenger for my maiden voyage. I remember thinking, "Let someone else with experience be responsible."

Around me on all sides were huge control panels and computer equipment, with buttons and switches and signals of every imaginable kind. For someone barely becoming acquainted with a computer, this was daunting. I was given a headset with large earphones. "Not to worry," I was told; I would be in touch with the command center throughout the flight as long as I kept the headset on and listened.

I grabbed the headset. Thankfully I could hear the voice of the instructor speaking to me. He welcomed me and called me by name, assuring me that he would be guiding me through the flight. He counseled, "Keep the headset on and listen for the instruction that will be forthcoming." I can assure you that I was quite willing to wear the headset, although I soon discovered it was not necessarily comfortable.

With my heart racing and my eyes glued on the indicators giving the minutes and seconds, I watched the countdown before blastoff into outer space. Five, four, three, two, one, and the rockets were fired. Gravity forced me to a ninety-degree angle against the back of the seat. I could hardly believe what I was experiencing. Catching my breath, I looked out the side window. It appeared that I was in fact speeding into outer space, far into the galaxy. There were others in the space shuttle with me, but I was at the controls, with the sense of an awesome responsibility.

I listened eagerly to the voice from the command

center telling me to hold tightly to the control stick and keep the shuttle traveling on the center line on the screen in front of me. The instruction was clear; carrying it out, however, proved a real challenge. It seemed impossible, try as I would, to hold exactly to the center line. Traveling off course even briefly at that speed could result in missing the target by millions of miles. In-flight course correction was essential and needed to be constant and continual throughout the flight.

By clinging white-knuckled to the control stick and keeping my eyes riveted on the center line in front of me, I could hold the course. I wanted to hear every word of instruction and warning, and I wanted to carry it out exactly, without variation in the slightest degree. Even though this was my first experience in "outer space," by listening and following the directions coming from the command center, I was able to bring the spaceship in right on target. What a relief! I was elated, and my fellow passengers cheered, "You did it, you did it!"

I frequently relive this remarkable experience in my mind. I realize more than ever before the importance of staying in communication with the command center, whatever it takes, at whatever the cost in discomfort or temporary uncertainty. The command center I speak of is not at the Houston Training Facility but is rather the voice of direction, guidance, warning, and comfort from the Holy Ghost that we can hear in our minds and our hearts. It is an infallible guide to which we have access while navigating the sometimes troubled waters of mortality. We are not like a ship without a rudder, tossed to and fro in times of storm. Rather, we have an inner compass, steady and dependable.

Communication with the Lord is a two-way process when we prepare ourselves to listen. Sometimes the impressions may come as a warm feeling that things will be all right. Other times we may receive specific direction. And there may be times when the message cannot get through because our receptivity to the Spirit is low. Distracted by the noise of the world, we may become deafened to the whisperings of the still, small voice.

I believe our Father in Heaven is often shouting to us, "I love you," but we may not hear because we have taken off our headsets. We can reestablish and strengthen that communication with the command center through weekly church attendance, which provides us with the opportunity to remember, renew, and recommit to the covenants we have made. Each time we partake of the sacred emblems of the sacrament, we renew our baptismal covenant that we will always remember the Lord and keep his commandments. When we do this, we have the promise that we can always have his Spirit to be with us, to direct us, to comfort us, and to warn us if we vary from the "center line," or the strait and narrow path. Constant course corrections will be necessary, but we can bring our ship in safely when we follow the counsel of our Guide.

For advanced training in navigating the journey of life, we can go to the temple. The ordinances and covenants we participate in there are our surest guide. They prepare us to see the whole path of eternity, enabling us to stay on course. In the temple, the noise of the world is left behind, and our ability to hear the voice of our teacher, the Holy Ghost, is greatly enhanced. What a blessing it is that we never need travel without guidance on our journey through mortality!

11

IS ANYBODY HOME?

At the risk of opening a floodgate of homesickness, I asked a sister missionary a question I thought would bring a short and spontaneous response: "What is your favorite room in your house when you are at home?" She paused and pondered while I waited.

"I guess I would have to go home," she said in a tone that suggested she had just made a quick return trip mentally before giving her answer. "I'd stand on the front porch and holler, 'Is anybody home?' If I heard my mom's voice coming from one of the rooms, that would be my favorite room."

A bit taken aback by her thoughtful response, I persisted, "But don't you have a favorite room—the kitchen, your bedroom, the family room, or even the patio?"

She wanted me to understand that my question required more than a quick and easy answer. "We have a nice house," she said, "but if Mom isn't there, it's just a house. It isn't home." She further explained, "I wouldn't need to see her. Just hearing her voice from any room would make it my favorite room." Her careful answer to my simple question has returned to my mind again and again.

Following one of the sessions of the rededication of the Cardston Temple in June 1991, after most of the crowd had left, a small group of us, including some General Authorities, were gathered in one of the beautiful rooms. The room, forty feet square, has a thirty-six-foot ceiling that is ornamentally plastered and decorated with gold leaf and stencil work. The wood finish is chiefly rich African mahogany, with inlays of ebony, rose, maple, and tulip woods in delicate patterns, showing remarkable craftsmanship. Each of the leaded windows is composed of 144 small panes of glass in different colors. It is a stunning place. But on this occasion, what we felt was greater by far than the splendor of the room. As we stood reverently trying to grasp the grandeur of the dedication experience, I heard one of the visiting authorities say in a soft voice, "All temples are the House of the Lord, but today I feel like I am in the home of our Father in Heaven." I shared the same feeling. On that occasion I felt sure He was home.

Often as I approach the temple, particularly in the early morning, I look up at the inscription on the outer wall. I think of many friends who have plaques near the doors of their homes identifying who lives there, and I read, "Holiness to the Lord, House of the Lord." I ponder, "Will I know if he is here today? Will he know I am here?"

Just inside the temple doors is a shallow pool surrounded by live plants with a massive stone carving depicting the woman at the well in Samaria. Beside her is a representation of the Savior, who went out of his way to teach her about the great plan of happiness and about living water that quenches spiritual thirst. It is interesting that he offered this teaching to a woman who likely would not even have been worthy of a temple recommend at that time in her life. The account in John tells us that she didn't recognize the Savior even though she was by his side at the well. She was not yet ready to grasp the significance of this remarkable experience, although she expressed some anticipation in these words: "I know that Messias cometh, which is called Christ: when he is come, he will tell us all things." I wonder how she must have felt when he told her, "I that speak unto thee am he" (John 4: 25–26). Surely, if he would go out of his way to teach the woman at Samaria, would he not come to his house to teach us if we went out of our way to be there?

And if he *was* trying to teach me, would I listen? Or might I be preoccupied and miss feeling his presence and learning what might be a customized tutoring intended for me that day? Could it be that I would miss him, even though he was there, because I was looking in the wrong place or using the wrong faculties to witness spiritual things? Nephi warned his distracted brothers, "Ye have heard his voice from time to time; and he hath spoken unto you in a still small voice, but ye were past feeling, that ye could not *feel* his words" (1 Nephi 17:45; emphasis added).

Might we ever miss opportunities for communion because we come with no expectation, no readiness? Following the resurrection of Christ, two of his disciples were walking toward the village of Emmaus. Jesus joined them, but, we are told, "their eyes were holden that they should not know him," even though they spoke with him and he with them. Later, when their eyes were opened and they knew him, they remembered, "Did not our heart burn within us, while he talked with us by the way?" (Luke 24:16, 32).

President Harold B. Lee, speaking at the British

Area Conference in Manchester, England, in August 1971, spoke of his experience with missionaries: "I have a session with the missionary groups as they go out, in the temple, where they are permitted to ask intimate questions that wouldn't be proper to be discussed elsewhere. They sometimes ask, could you tell us a certain place in the temple where the Savior has been seen? My answer is, keep in mind that this is The House of the Lord; this is the place that we try to keep as pure and holy and sacred as any building we have. This is the most likely place he would come when he comes on earth. Don't ask for a certain place because he has walked these halls."

Elder John A. Widtsoe addressed this matter, which is of great importance if we are to understand what we might expect in our temple experience and to prepare ourselves for the opportunities available in this holy place. He wrote, "It is a great promise that to the temples God will come and that in them man shall see God. What does this promised communion mean? Does it mean that once in a while God may come into the temples, and that once in a while the pure in heart who go into the temples, may, there, by the spirit of God, always have a wonderfully rich communion with God? I think that is what it means to me and to you and to most of us. We have gone into these holy houses, with our minds freed from the ordinary earthly cares, and have literally felt the presence of God. In this way, the temples are always places where God manifests himself to man and increases his intelligence. A temple is a place of revelation" (*Utah Genealogical and Historical Magazine*, April 1921, 56).

Through revelation concerning the temple we read, "Behold, I have accepted this house, and my name shall be here; and I will manifest myself to my people in mercy in this house" (D&C 110:7).

It has been years since I learned from a sister missionary that grand lesson about calling from the front porch, "Is anybody home?" and listening anxiously for a response. Sitting peacefully in the chapel of the temple, while listening to sacred organ music, thinking, pondering, and praying, I am tempted to call out, or at least to whisper, "Is anybody home?" When I listen carefully and prayerfully, I feel my heart burn within. I know this is his house. I *feel* he is there.

12

A SMALL
WHITE PILLOW

*P*icture an old trunk in an attic. It may be filled with treasures, the tokens of fascinating stories left untold. Children of a later generation may sort through these items unknowingly, not understanding the meaning and value of the precious memories they represent. What mysteries might be unfolded if they only understood?

One day, someone sorting through my things may come upon a small pillow, about four to six inches square, made with what appears to be old, used, washed and rewashed fabric edged with a border of worn lace. They might be perplexed by a little pillow not soft to the touch but rather firm and hard on the surface. Examining it even carefully would not reveal a reason for its preservation.

Lest the story of that small white pillow should one day become a mystery, I shall tell it now.

While on assignment for the Church, representing

Young Women, my travels took me to the great city of Lima, Peru. Although it was a bustling place, with many people coming and going, signs of deep poverty were everywhere. My hosts explained to me that in some areas on Sundays one member of the family has to remain at home while the others go to church. If no one is left in their humble home, chances are they will be robbed of even what little they have. Yet, although those people are poor, they are rich in the things not of this world.

I was taught in a remarkable way by a master teacher in a humble classroom where a small group of young women were meeting one Sunday morning. The teacher, who appeared to be no older than her students, began the lesson. "We are children of our Heavenly Father," she said in a tone of profound conviction. The eyes of the young women sitting in front of her revealed absolute trust in that eternal truth. They knew it was true, or at least they believed that their young teacher knew. The teacher continued, "The lesson manual suggests that you each take a piece of paper and a pencil and write your name on it and the statement, 'I am a child of God.' Since we have only one piece of paper and one small pencil, I have written the sentence across the top of the page. I will pass the paper and pencil. *If you feel like it,* write your name as an indication that you know who you really are." She handed the paper and well-used pencil to the first young woman on the end of the bench.

I watched these young women, with their beautiful dark skin and hair, while each in turn added her name as a testimony of her faith. Not one of them hesitated for even an instant. I pondered, "Who are these young women really?" In that humble setting, in the world but not part of the world, I wondered if I might qualify to have my name added with theirs to that small piece of paper.

Could girls this young realize, even in part, the grand work unfolding in their land in such a remarkable way? My question was answered the following day as we stood together, these young women and I, with sawdust at our feet on the foundation and subflooring of the Lima Peru Temple. There were skilled laborers and craftsmen, engineers and foremen, each contributing a part from the foundation to the pinnacle of what would become the House of the Lord. Other builders were also at work. Theirs were longer hours, with a different kind of pay, but their tasks were essential if the purpose of the temple was to be realized. These were the faithful parents and leaders, friends and teachers, whose prayers and study and sacrifice had contributed to a strong foundation of faith in the lives of these young women and other youth like them.

As I listened to the young women speak with excitement and conviction about *their* temple, I realized that their spiritual age far exceeded the number of years they had spent in this earth life. Perhaps they were remembering.

Time was short. Deep feelings of friendship had so quickly developed as we were bonded together in spirit in the gospel of Jesus Christ. I would leave Peru and these dear friends, perhaps never to see them again in mortality. We said our good-byes amid tears of gratitude and tenderness of heart and a resolve to the soul.

In the midst of the sawdust under the framework of the temple, my new friends reverently placed into my hands a small white pillow. Immediately one of the young women began to explain, perhaps to ensure my appreciation for a gift whose value may not have been obvious. "This pillow," she said with some emotion, reaching out to touch it as if to retain the treasure just a bit longer, "is stuffed with sawdust from *our* temple." The young women standing together watched anxiously to see if I really liked their gift. My thought was, did they realize how precious it was? Did they realize its value?

In my mind I could see generation after generation coming to this temple in Peru, where the ordinances would be given under priesthood authority. These young women would be sealed in the temple, their children and their children's children born under the covenant for generations to come. The vision opened to my mind of past generations listed on family file cards, their names being spoken in the temple by proxies who would open the doors for them.

The pillow was much more than a pillow. It would serve as a reminder as I looked beyond its surface to try to comprehend the sacrifice, the blessings, the meaning of the temple in the lives of these faithful Saints. And someday, I hope whoever finds the little white pillow in my drawer will recognize its worth as a symbol. It may not have any value in the currency of the world. But its symbolic reminder will be priceless to all who know its story.

13

A REFUGE IN
TIMES OF STORM

*N*O ADMITTANCE. ABSOLUTELY NO ENTRY. KEEP OUT! These strong words were printed in large, bold, block letters across the door at the rear of a popular Chinese restaurant where Heber and I were going to eat. There was no mistake about the clarity, the intent, or the expectation from such direction. We had not a moment of hesitation about whether or not we would enter that door.

What if we could mark the doors of our homes with such direction and conviction to keep out unwanted influences? What markings could we use to protect our homes and families from unwanted intrusions?

Marking doors is not a new practice. In the book of Exodus the children of Israel were instructed to mark their doors with the blood of a lamb without blemish, symbolic of the atoning blood of Christ, for a protection against the destroyer: "When he seeth the blood upon the lintel, and on the two side posts, the Lord will pass over the door, and will not suffer the destroyer to come in unto your houses to smite you" (Exodus 12:23).

This event in history holds a message for our day, when concern for our homes and families increases as the powers and influences of the adversary threaten to destroy all that is precious. Today some well-meaning parents, anxious to provide security for their families, may put locks on their doors, motion sensors in their yards, smoke detectors in their bedrooms, security systems to sound alarms in case of intrusion, and double-paned glass on their windows to keep out the storms. Although these efforts certainly have their place and should not be ignored, they do not come close to protecting against the greatest threat of our day. President Gordon B. Hinckley has warned, "We live in a season of wickedness, pornography, immorality. All of the sins of Sodom and Gomorrah haunt our society. Our young people have never faced a greater challenge. We have never seen more clearly the lecherous face of evil" (*Ensign*, November 2001, 6).

Too often, after all the protection we have provided for our families' physical safety and well-being, we open our homes to the negative influences of the world, turning on the television without discretion, bringing in popular but questionable videos, surfing the Internet for enticing influences that can ravage our otherwise safe places, and decorating our walls with symbols of the world.

A storm is raging. It is no ordinary storm—not the kind where you can lock the windows and secure the doors and be safe inside. This storm of evil comes in through the airwaves and the media; it is tracked in from the workplace and even the playground.

But if we are prepared we need not fear. Like the children of Israel, we are given guidance for the protection of our homes and our families so the destroying enemy will pass us by. We must write, not with blood, as the children of Israel, but as Paul says, "not with ink, but with the Spirit of the living God; not in tables of stone, but in fleshy tables of the heart" (2 Corinthians 3:3). When our hearts are attuned to the Spirit of the living God and our homes are marked by that Spirit, therein lies our safety.

Each time we approach the door to the temple, the Lord's House, we meet an authorized person stationed there to verify our worthiness to enter. Those bearing the proper identification may pass. Without this recommend, this document of authorization and worthiness, there is "no admittance." Such screening serves as a filter to strain out, wherever possible, any impurities that might weaken not the building but the Spirit within it, the source of power, revelation, inspiration, comfort, peace, hope, and promise.

Suppose this analogy could be brought to bear upon our homes. Could we have a family filter through which the outside influences of the world must pass before entrance is permitted? Could every family member be enlisted in this great responsibility to stand guard in screening what is permitted within the walls of our homes? Each one can ask, "Will this activity, this attitude, this language, this program, this music, this influence in any way endanger our safe place or lessen the Spirit in our home?" And if the answer is yes—or even maybe—that family member, young or old, can shout, "No admittance. Absolutely no entry. Keep out!"

Regular attendance at the temple gives parents an increased sensitivity to that Spirit that will help them stand guard against evil influences. Elder John A. Widtsoe gave this great promise: "Spiritual power is generated within temple walls, and sent out to bless the church fitted for its reception by participating in temple privileges. The path from the temple to the home of man is divinely brilliant. Every home penetrated by the spirit enlightens, cheers, and comforts every member of the household. The peace we covet is found in such homes" (*Improvement Era*, April 1936, 228).

Participation in the ordinances and covenants of the temple provides a reminder of the eternal nature of family ties. Homes that are blessed with those promises partake of an increased spirit of love and reverence. Reverence is a powerful tool for filtering out disruptive intrusion and contention that might interrupt communication. And love has great power, as the Prophet Joseph Smith taught: "Nothing is so much calculated to lead people to forsake sin as to take them by the hand, and watch over them with tenderness. When persons manifest the least kindness and love to me, O what power it has over my mind, while the opposite course has a tendency to harrow up all the harsh feelings and depress the human mind" (*Teachings of the Prophet Joseph Smith* [Salt Lake City: Deseret Book, 1976], 240).

Families committed to striving for such love and reverence in their homes, protecting themselves with a "filter" that will screen out any unwanted intrusions, might well have a foretaste of the Millennium even now. As President George Q. Cannon taught, "By the Saints refusing to be led by the influences of Satan and not yielding to his seductive temptations, he is virtually bound so far as they are concerned; and, when the head of the family can attain unto this power and persuade his wife and family to do likewise, the power of Satan will be bound in that habitation, and the Millennium will have commenced in that household" (*Gospel Truth* [Salt Lake City: Deseret Book, 1987], 1:88).

As we bring the influence and spirit of the temple into our homes, our homes will be a refuge in times of storm. The negative influences of the world will find no place in our homes: "No admittance. Absolutely no entry. Keep out!"

14

TRIED AND TESTED

I have come to believe there are no coincidences in the temple. You don't just "happen to be" where you should be. You may feel to set aside reason and schedule, habit and assignment, with seemingly no explanation. Later, when the explanation becomes apparent, you consider with a feeling of anxiety what you might have missed if you were not where you happened to be at a particular time. I had such an experience walking through the baptistry of the temple in the late afternoon on March 20, 2001.

On that day, in the foyer just outside the baptistry, two girls who looked to be around thirteen and fourteen years of age were standing with their leader. This is not unusual; there are often youth and their leaders in this location, either waiting to perform baptisms or having just finished and waiting for others in their group. It is easy to identify whether the work has been done or will yet be done by the condition of their hair.

On this occasion, street clothes and wet hair confirmed that the girls' mission at the temple this late afternoon was complete and they were about ready to leave. I felt impressed to detain these two young women and their leader. I invited them to take a seat on the bench nearby, and I pulled up a chair so we might have a little visit. They appeared surprised but were quite willing to respond.

It is common to speak to youth groups in the chapel, before they change into white clothing. This gives us an opportunity to express gratitude for their work in the temple and hopefully to help them feel the importance of the ordinances they are doing in behalf of others. We also often chat with them while they wait their turn to be called to the font. I don't remember ever before having detained any youth at the time they were ready to leave.

The conversation began with the usual questions: "Tell me your names." "Where are you from?" "Is this your first time doing baptisms for the dead?" It was immediately evident that this was not to be a routine conversation. This trip to the temple was an experience these young women and their leader would remember for a lifetime, and so would I. Their story of courage, determination, trials, and tests began to unfold.

Sister Tammy Bromley, a dedicated twenty-eight-year-old wife and mother of three little boys, lived in Prince Rupert, a beautiful area in the far northern part of the province of British Columbia. She admitted sometimes feeling tired but never bored. Then one day, quite unexpectedly, her responsibility was to increase. Near the end of August 2000, she received a call from the branch president to be the Young Women leader in the Prince Rupert Branch. This may not have seemed like a major responsibility, since there were only four young women in the entire branch—two sisters from a single-parent family and two others who at this time didn't even attend. "I fell in love with those girls the minute I received my calling," she was quick to explain, adding, "Into my heart and mind loomed a feeling of a major responsibility." The words of President Hinckley weighed heavily on Sister Bromley's mind: "When a girl is saved, a generation is saved" (*New Era*, September 1988, 44).

Early in the year, plans had been made for a trip to the Cardston Alberta Temple during the first week in September. The trip would require a twenty-five hour drive each way. Sister Bromley felt that this opportunity was a must for these young women who lived so far from other LDS youth. Yet, having just received her calling in August, she was left with too little time to make arrangements to be gone for several days. She felt that she could not take the girls, and they could not go without her. However, this obstacle was not to deprive these young women of the opportunity to take part in the sacred temple work. She made a promise to "her girls": During the spring break they would take the twenty-five-hour drive to the temple. "I was determined to get them there, no matter what," she explained. "We talked and we planned. Each week we would recite the Young Women theme emphasizing the last lines: ' . . . prepare to make and keep sacred covenants, receive the ordinances of the temple, and enjoy the blessings of exaltation.'

"When there is something that might change a life, save a soul, or bless a youth, it seems there is so often opposition," explained this faithful leader. "As the March day approached and our anticipation was rising, our plans, made so well in advance, started to crumble. I learned two weeks before the day of departure that the counselor who was going to take one of the girls in her car had had a change of plans and needed to leave a week early. The Young Men president, who had considered coming along to help with transportation, decided it was not a good time for him.

"We turned to the Lord," she explained. "We fasted and prayed, and the girls received priesthood blessings. Nothing was going to stop us." Sister Bromley was still smiling but her mood soon changed, and the two young women sitting beside their leader listened intently as if hearing the details of this saga for the first time. "In a minivan we managed to squish the five members of our family and my two young women, plus enough luggage for each of us for one week."

At this point she launched into the story of their long journey. Hearing some of the details of their excursion, I felt at times that I was riding with them. I learned that Sister Bromley's nine-month-old baby suffers from a chronic medical condition; his kidneys and bladder do not function properly. This little caravan traveled nine hours the first day with "an extremely sick baby" and thirteen hours the second day, arriving at Sister Bromley's father's place in Bassano (approximately three hours from the temple) around 9:00 P.M. Saturday night.

On Sunday morning they all went to church, but by evening the baby's condition had become more serious. Brother and Sister Bromley took him to the emergency room at the hospital and there learned that he had a urinary infection and strep throat.

Surely this would justify abandoning the trip, at least for this time, but this was not even a consideration for Sister Bromley and her supportive husband. They had an appointment to be at the temple Tuesday morning, and nothing was going to stop them. They did not have any idea at this time of the opposition that was yet to come.

On Monday the girls, seeing that Sister Bromley's father had horses, were eager to go horseback riding. Hannah, the older of the two sisters, said that she was an experienced rider. She mounted the horse selected for her and started off down a gravel road. The horse, not reined in, took off like lightning, and Hannah was thrown into a ditch, landing on her head. Sister Bromley's husband and father were both there immediately to give her a priesthood blessing before rushing her to the hospital.

The love Sister Bromley felt for these girls was evident as she put her arm around Hannah, who was sitting next to her on the bench. The story went on: "She complained that her head hurt and she had no feeling in her legs. She was barely conscious, and they used special c-spine equipment to get her from the car on a stretcher and into the ambulance. In the hospital, X rays were taken immediately. We waited anxiously in the emergency room for about two hours in silent prayer until the doctor came with the report. There were no broken bones and only a minor shock to the spine, which had caused the feeling of numbness in her legs. Hannah was already up and walking, but they insisted on keeping her in the hospital overnight for observation.

"By this time," Sister Bromley said, "I was losing confidence and beginning to question the reasons we were there and even to doubt if it was the right thing to have come. I felt like I needed some kind of a sign or revelation to know if we should continue on our journey to the temple. As I walked into my father's house, Erin, Hannah's younger sister, was sitting on the couch writing in her journal. Her first comment was, 'We're still going to the temple, right?' Those words stung in my heart. 'Yes, we're going,' I told her. But at this point I had no idea of the continued opposition we would face."

In Taber, about one and a half hours before they would reach their destination, they stopped to drop off the two older boys at the sitter's and pick up her husband's niece to tend the sick baby. They also stopped for gasoline. The cost of gas had recently skyrocketed and was a heavy drain on their limited budget.

Sister Bromley continued with further details. "We were afraid we were going to be late for our appointment at the temple. My husband tried and tried but could not get the gas cap off. He finally pried it off and then couldn't put it back on. We used a diaper to cover the opening and were on our way for the last lap of our journey, hoping we would not be late for our appointment, the whole reason for the trip."

They were getting closer, but the tests were not over. The southern Alberta wind was howling fiercely, as it so often does in March, and strong gusts of wind blew against the van. They had a car topper that they had borrowed to help carry the luggage. They noticed as several cars passed that people were looking out their windows and pointing at the top of the little van. The force of the wind had blown the car topper loose. They pulled over and stopped to anchor it down. The fierceness of the wind blew the straps loose a second time, and once again they had to stop to fasten the car topper.

Sister Bromley said with tears in her eyes, "I felt if we could just get inside the temple, all would be well." She paused, looking at her girls and then at me.

Sitting close to her girls, this dedicated leader testified, "When I watched my two young women all in white climb the stairs, step down into the water, and participate in this sacred ordinance of baptism, I knew we had done the right thing. But I was anxious that the girls not be disappointed, that they would feel good about this experience regardless of our challenges. I had a prayer in my heart. Then as we walked out of the changing room, ready to leave the temple, we saw you, Sister Kapp, standing in the doorway by the font. You seemed so excited to see us even though you didn't know we were coming to the temple, and we were excited to see you. You said you would like to visit with us"—she raised both hands and finished her story—"and here we are!"

The spirit around this little assemblage in the House of the Lord was very strong. I felt at that moment that my "happening to be there" was not for the girls to hear what I might have to say but rather to hear the strong testimony of their leader in this setting at this time. "Tell me, Sister Bromley," I asked, "how did you continue on and on through such opposition and adversity? How did you do it?"

In the presence of these two young women, she bore a testimony that was confirmed by the Spirit and will be with "her girls" forever: "I am grateful for the strength of my husband, who has been a beacon of light and support through this whole experience. He is serving in the branch presidency, and it has been a blessing to have the strength of a priesthood holder traveling with us. He never complained."

She continued, "When I was twelve years old, my Young Women leader brought me to the temple to do baptisms for the dead. I have never forgotten that experience. It had a great impact on my young life. I did it partly for her, trusting it will do the same for my girls." Observing the expression on the faces of these young women, I felt her desire was assured. They would never forget their teacher, this experience, or her final few words: "I love my girls, and I love the Lord."

To help confirm in the minds of these weary travelers the importance of the grand work they had done, and to thank them for their endurance, I shared with them the message of President Hinckley in speaking to a group of youth in Guayaquil, Ecuador:

"When you are twelve years of age you may go to the Lord's house and there stand as a living proxy in behalf of someone who is dead. What a marvelous thing that is that you, an ordinary boy or girl, can stand in the place of some man or woman who at one time lived upon the earth, but who is now powerless to move forward without the blessing that you can give him or her. . . . There is no greater blessing that you can have than to stand as a proxy in a great service to those who have gone beyond" (Guayaquil, Ecuador, July 31, 1999).

Is it ever too far?

15

DON'T FORGET ME

I have told and retold the account of a young woman who wrote to me following a meeting in the British Isles where several hundred people were in the audience. "Do you remember me?" she wrote. "I was the one in the green jumper on the second row." No one wants to be forgotten, not now, not ever. Even a common flower carries the name "forget-me-not" as a reminder of a desire that is bone-marrow deep within each of us.

When the time came for us to leave our home in the spirit world to dwell for a time on earth, with all the excitement of this grand and important adventure, we shouted for joy. It seems reasonable to suppose that, as we were bidding our farewells to those who would follow after us into mortality, our parting thoughts would include the request "Please don't forget me." It is painful, even frightening, to consider the possibility that we would or could ever be left out, forgotten, or overlooked in matters that would affect our happiness now and for all eternity.

This is well illustrated in an account given by President Edward J. Wood of the Cardston Alberta Temple. While sealing a group of children to their parents, in the midst of the ceremony he felt an impression to ask the mother, "Sister, does this list contain the names of all your children?" She said yes, and he began again, but once more he stopped and asked if the list named all of her children. She told him there were no more children. He attempted to proceed, but a third time he was impelled to ask: "My sister, have you lost a child whose name is not on this list?" Then she said: "Yes, I do remember now. We did lose a little baby. It was born alive and died soon after. I had forgotten to put its name down." The name was given, and then that child, being the firstborn, was named first, and all were sealed to the parents. President Wood said, "Every time I started to seal the children I heard a voice say, 'Mother, don't forget me,' and I could not go any further. The appeal was made each time until the omission was discovered" (Melvin J. Ballard, *Crusader for Righteousness* [Salt Lake City: Bookcraft, 1966], 254).

One morning I related this account to some of the

ordinance workers in the Cardston Temple. When I finished, there were tears in the eyes of many and an expression of disbelief in the eyes of others, questioning how a mother could forget her child. A sister in the room spoke up in behalf of this mother who had seemingly forgotten her baby. She was anxious to explain that, according to her grandmother, who had been present on that occasion years ago, this dear sister was stricken with years and with some of the infirmities of old age. She was elderly; she had given birth to eighteen children. This quieted the concerns of those who struggled with even the thought that a mother could forget her child.

There are thousands upon thousands of souls who have preceded us through this mortal sojourn of life, who are living beyond the veil. They are hoping not to be forgotten. Those names on family file cards or temple file cards for whom we serve as proxies in performing their temple ordinances are much more than names on a card. They are people, our brothers and sisters, our relatives and others who will one day be our dear friends.

I have an older sister, Uvada, who lived only two days and died before I was born. I couldn't have forgotten her because I don't remember her in the first place. Or do I? The reality of an older sister comes to my mind and into my heart with a feeling of reverence and excitement as I find myself in the temple quietly pondering our family relationship. I am touched to know that I have an older sister who, I believe, remembers me even if I don't remember her in the way we commonly think of remembering.

When those we love, especially family members, are called home and we are left behind, we feel a sense of longing to be in touch. We feel in the depth of our hearts that we will never, ever forget them. But do they remember us? I pondered for some time after my father's passing: "Does he think of me? Does he know what I am doing?" One day, into my mind and my heart came his voice as surely as he had spoken to me in days gone by: "My dear, you have your privacy, but I know all the important things." I believe this.

President Joseph F. Smith had a deep understanding of such spiritual things and gives us an assurance that we are not forgotten. He writes of our loved ones beyond the veil: "If we can see, by the enlightening influence of the Spirit of God and through the words that have been spoken by the holy prophets of God, beyond the veil that separates us from the spirit world, surely those who have passed beyond, can see more clearly through the veil back here to us than it is possible for us to see to them from our sphere of action. . . . We are not separated from them. . . . We cannot forget them: we do not cease to love them; we always hold them in our hearts, in memory, and thus we are associated and united to them by ties that we cannot break, that we cannot dissolve or free ourselves from. . . . I claim that we live in their presence, they see us, they are solicitous for our welfare, they love us now more than ever. . . . They see the temptations and the evils that beset us in life, and the proneness of mortal beings to yield to temptation and wrong doing; hence their solicitude for us and their love for us and their desire for our well being must be greater than that which we feel for ourselves." (*Gospel Doctrine*, 5th ed. [Salt Lake City: Deseret Book, 1939], 430–31).

There may be occasions when, for whatever reason, we feel left out, overlooked, or forgotten—but we are not. The Lord will never forget us. He assures us in these comforting words: "Can a woman forget her sucking child, that she should not have compassion on the son of her womb? Yea, they may forget, yet will I not forget thee. . . . Behold, I have graven thee upon the palms of my hands; thy walls are continually before me" (1 Nephi 21:15–16).

He will not forget us or our loved ones, not ever. Let us return often to the temple and demonstrate there that we too will never forget those who have gone on before us.

16

THE PRISONERS
SHALL GO FREE

I presented a photo ID card to the uniformed guard at the gate. He examined it carefully, looking down at the card and then up at me. Without a smile or a greeting, he pushed a button, and the heavy steel gates behind him began opening. I wasn't sure I wanted to proceed, but I had made a commitment, so I continued on, hearing the solid clanging sound as the gates closed behind me. Presenting my identification one more time to a less-imposing officer, I waited as he activated two large doors by some electronic means. An attendant was motioned to accompany me to my appointment in the state prison, where I had been asked to speak to the inmates. I was ushered down the wide hall with metal grills on window-like openings on either side. Men who appeared to be security guards were stationed all along the way.

Approaching the inner part of the prison, I could hear the faint sound of music, beautiful male voices singing four-part harmony in soft tones. The heavy cloud that had engulfed me in this foreign environment lifted. I recognized the song, a familiar hymn that seemed most unlikely in such a setting. Standing in the doorway of the chapel, I was warmly greeted by the leader who had asked me to participate in this gathering. We waited while the men in dark-blue jumpsuits, holding the familiar green hymnbooks, finished singing all of the verses of hymn number 125, "How Gentle God's Commands":

> *How gentle God's commands!*
> *How kind his precepts are!*
> *Come, cast your burdens on the Lord*
> *And trust his constant care.*
>
> *Beneath his watchful eye,*
> *His Saints securely dwell;*
> *That hand which bears all nature up*
> *Shall guard his children well.*
>
> *Why should this anxious load*
> *Press down your weary mind?*
> *Haste to your Heav'nly Father's throne*
> *And sweet refreshment find.*
>
> *His goodness stands approved,*
> *Unchanged from day to day;*
> *I'll drop my burden at his feet*
> *And bear a song away.*

In this setting, I contemplated with a deeper sense of appreciation the invitation to drop our burden at his feet.

Following the meeting, one of the younger men reached out his hand and introduced himself. "I'm Brother _____," he said in a quiet tone. I took his hand, looked into his eyes, wondered about his family, and thought, "My brother, when did the chains that bind begin to enslave you? Where were your good friends who might have strengthened you when you were succumbing to the grasp of the adversary?"

I left the prison with a deeper sense of the limitations and burdens of prison life, as well as a new appreciation of and gratitude for freedom. A few days following my visit to the state prison, I received a handwritten letter expressing appreciation for my visit and saying, "Thanks for giving us hope." The letter was signed, "From your friends, the men in blue," and each of their signatures was included.

One of the prisoners, a man with a family, had been confined for several years, serving a sentence for fraud, I was told. Realizing the consequences of his actions, he grasped at any opportunity to make restitution for the wrong choices that had led him to the misuse of funds. He had been taught the gospel of

Jesus Christ, the worth of a soul, and the blessings of the Atonement, but could that apply to him in his restrictive, confining, limiting condition? Could the atonement of Jesus Christ reach into a prison? The words of President Boyd K. Packer make it very clear: "Save for those few who defect to perdition . . . , there is no habit, no addiction, no rebellion, no transgression, no offense exempted from the promise of complete forgiveness" (*Ensign*, November 1995, 19).

This prisoner believed in the atonement of Jesus Christ. He believed in the grace of God. He believed the words of the Savior given to the Prophet Joseph Smith in revelation: "Behold, he who has repented of his sins, the same is forgiven, and I, the Lord, remember them no more. By this ye may know if a man repenteth of his sins—behold, he will confess them and forsake them" (D&C 58:42–43). He must have found great comfort in the words from Isaiah: "Come now, and let us reason together, saith the Lord: though your sins be as scarlet, they shall be as white as snow; though they be red like crimson, they shall be as wool" (Isaiah 1:18).

This inmate realized the profound blessing made possible by the Savior, our advocate with the Father, who is pleading our cause that we may have everlasting life (see D&C 45:3). He knew that in time he would be released from prison, but he sought a greater freedom. He needed the atonement of Jesus Christ to do for him what he could not do for himself if he was ever to find happiness and be united with his family forever.

Looking out beyond the prison walls, beyond the heavy metal doors and barred windows and the law that restrained him for a time, his thoughts turned to others who were held in prison through no fault of their own—a prison of a different kind. There are people—good, righteous people—who are held captive in what is referred to as spirit prison until their temple ordinances are performed for them on earth. Many great and noble people who died without a knowledge of the gospel have been taught in the spirit world but must wait until someone searches their records, finds their names, and serves as a proxy for them, doing for them what they cannot do for themselves.

This prisoner, serving his time, occupied himself in a most commendable way. His heart was turned to his fathers. He became involved with the opportunities made available by the Church through the Family History Center in the prison. When the time came for him to be released, he had family file cards that represented months and months of devotion, dedication, determination, faith, and love that penetrated the veil.

One memorable evening after this man had been out of prison for some time and proper steps had been taken for restitution through the atonement of Christ, he was prepared once again to enter the temple. He sat in the sealing room with family members and a couple of friends he had asked to be there to act with him as proxies for family file names he had uncovered through his labors in the prison. As the temple ordinances were being performed for each name, it was evident in the minds and hearts of everyone present that these were more than names on a card. They were family members being released from spirit prison, their release made possible by a family member who had searched their names while serving his time in prison. That evening in the sealing room, the "welding link" through the keys, powers, and authority of the priesthood and the blessings of the Atonement penetrated every heart.

Standing on the hill as we left the temple that evening, the words of the Prophet Joseph Smith filled my mind: "Brethren, shall we not go on in so great a cause? . . . Courage, brethren; and on, on to the victory!

Let your hearts rejoice, and be exceedingly glad. Let the earth break forth into singing. Let the dead speak forth anthems of eternal praise to the King Immanuel, who hath ordained, before the world was, that which would enable us to redeem them out of their prison; for the prisoners shall go free" (D&C 128:22).

17

NO MORE STRANGERS

They were new to the area. They were new to the country. They had found their way to the church—not just any church, but The Church of Jesus Christ of Latter-day Saints.

October 24, 1999, was just an ordinary Sunday, or so it seemed to the Saints gathered on that day. But not for this couple. On that morning a black man and woman speaking only French walked through the doors of an LDS chapel in Florida. They were too late for sacrament meeting; members had already dispersed to their respective classes, and only one or two adults lingered in the foyer. These stragglers were trying unsuccessfully to bridge the language gap in an attempt to communicate with the strangers. The bishop was summoned. He was quite willing to welcome these strangers, but not knowing if they were investigators, less-active members, visitors, or someone seeking financial assistance (as is sometimes the case with drop-ins), he tried to inquire about their visit to the ward. The language barrier continued to be a real problem in getting any message through.

What might such a couple do in a situation where they didn't speak the language, didn't know anyone, needed help, and wanted to be accepted and trusted? What credentials did they have that might open doors in this time of need when they were unable to communicate in a language that could be understood? In desperation they were prompted to find a resolution. Reaching into their pockets, they each drew out a small card and presented it to the bishop. It was not a business card, not a credit card, but a small card that instantly revealed their identity, their commitment, their righteousness, and their faith. No translation was necessary. The bishop immediately recognized their current temple recommends. Without further explanation or delay, doors and hearts were opened.

A French-speaking member was called out of the Gospel Doctrine class. She soon translated the couple's story. Because of the political upheaval in their native land of Haiti, and their prominent position in the community, they had been forced to flee for their lives. They were uprooted, unsettled—strangers in a foreign land. Although they had escaped the risk that would have been associated with their plight if they had stayed in their own country, what of the uncertainty in the situation they were now facing? It was an interesting coincidence that the sister called out of class to translate *just happened* to be an attorney specializing in immigration procedures. This couple were no longer strangers. They found themselves embraced by brothers and sisters willing to assist and anxious to offer a refuge, a welcome, a safe place in a ward family.

And why was I present to observe this miracle? The Saturday afternoon prior to this Sabbath day, an impressive annual event had taken place at the church. The sisters in the stake Relief Society had gathered in a conference in which the theme of the day had focused on becoming true disciples, reaching out to others in all circumstances, and remembering that "when ye are in the service of your fellow beings ye are only in the service of your God" (Mosiah 2:17). I had come to participate in that women's conference.

The message delivered at the conference seemed to be well received, but the application of the message, as exemplified by the actions of the Saints in this ward, was a sermon that paled any words spoken the previous day. The profound impact of being in the service of our brothers and sisters was played out in a dramatic way as we witnessed this divine truth: "Ye are no more strangers and foreigners, but fellowcitizens with the saints, and of the household of God" (Ephesians 2:19).

There are times when obedience to counsel from a prophet of God places us in a position to receive answers to our prayers and blessings from the Lord. President Howard W. Hunter is remembered for this strong admonition: "I . . . invite the members of the Church to establish the temple of the Lord as the great symbol of their membership and the supernal setting for their most sacred covenants. It would be the deepest desire of my heart to have every member of the Church be temple worthy. I would hope that every adult member would be worthy of—and carry— a current temple recommend, even if proximity to a temple does not allow immediate or frequent use of it" (*Ensign*, July 1994, 5).

A current temple recommend requires no translation and tells the whole story of the bearer's identity. We have taken upon us our Master's name, and in so doing we become fellow citizens with the Saints.

18

A PLACE OF HOPE
AND PROMISE

*M*y mother played in a dance band when she was young and had a beautiful alto voice. She didn't read music but played by ear. I remember the Sunday afternoons when we were waiting for Dad to return home from his bishop's responsibilities. She would sit at our upright piano over in the corner of the living room and play for hours. I loved the peace I felt when I heard my mother sing and play.

Mom had two favorite songs, and whatever else she added from her repertoire on any given day, including numbers with a swing—a carryover from her dance-band days—she always included those two, "Whispering Hope" and "In the Garden." I remember that corner of the room being filled with what to me was a feeling of *hope* and *promise*. I hear her full, rich alto voice even now:

> *I come to the Garden alone*
> *While the dew is still on the roses.*

And the voice I hear falling on my ear
The Son of God discloses.

And he walks with me,
And he talks with me,
And he tells me I am his own,
And the joys we share
As we tarry there,
None other has ever known.

—CHARLES AUSTIN MILES

In our world today there is chaos and turmoil, uncertainty and sorrow, ample reason for despair and depression and a loss of equilibrium. The media speaks of a wake-up call, an attack, but the prophet speaks of hope and promise. "The battle with the evil one will go on and on and on," he warns. "It will rise against the Church. It will rise against you individually. It will be felt in the future as it has been in the past." What is his response to this crisis? "Keep the temple as busy or busier than it has been. The Lord will bless you and you will be happier. I make a promise to you that every time you come to the temple you will be a better man or woman when you leave than you were when you came. That is a promise. I believe it with all my heart" (*Church News*, January 29, 2000).

In the temple we learn more of the great plan of

happiness and our reason for unwavering hope. We learn of the promises in relation to our covenants, and we feel God's binding love. We might feel as five-year-old Adam James did when his father asked, "Adam, do you know Heavenly Father loves you?"

Without hesitation he responded, "Yes."

"How do you know?" his father asked.

"He tells me in my mind to know."

The conversation continued: "But you can't see him."

"But he can see me."

"What if someone says you can't know?"

The child spoke again the truth he could feel: "He tells me in my mind to know."

There are times when that assurance is absolutely essential to our survival if we are not only to endure but also to enjoy our journey through this mortal life. The holy temple is our refuge, our home away from home. Our love of God and faith in his promises through our temple covenants can provide a quiet, inner peace in the most extreme disruptions and disappointments in our lives. We may sometimes forget that these covenants we make with him include binding promises from him to us, as explained by President George Q. Cannon: "When we . . . covenanted with our Father in heaven to serve Him and keep His commandments, He bound Himself also by covenant to us that He would never desert us, never leave us to ourselves, never forget us, that in the midst of trials and hardships, when everything was arrayed against us, He would be near unto us and would sustain us. That was His covenant" (*Gospel Truth* [Salt Lake City: Deseret Book, 1987], 1:170).

It is one thing to study and believe, but when put to the test, will we find that our foundation is truly grounded and rooted in the promises of our temple covenants? Can we survive the high winds, the storms, the extreme heat? When we feel like a young plant stripped of our leaves and battered to the ground by hail, will we be able to rise again and again?

One day in the local news I read of the tragedy of a father and son who drowned together. The obituary read, in part, "A duck hunting outing turned into disaster Saturday, Oct. 13, after choppy water and heavy winds capsized a boat on Scofield Reservoir and a father and son from Ephraim drowned. Larry and Trevor went hand in hand to meet Larry and Janet's youngest son LJ. They were also preceded in death by Larry's father and his younger sister Sharese."

But that is only part of the story. The human

drama, the story of the incredible circumstances that preceded this tragedy, was not included in the obituary and would hardly have been believed if it had been.

Wilda Thompson, a widow, stood with quiet serenity as friends and neighbors filed by on the day of the funeral to express their love and support at this time of sorrow in the loss of her son and grandson. What many did not know was that this courageous woman was already well seasoned with sorrow and tragedy.

Wilda is my first cousin. Our mothers were sisters, and we lived in the same small town during some of our growing-up years. As children we played together, although Wilda was much younger than I. When her older sister tap-danced in a Shirley Temple costume with Shirley Temple ringlets bouncing to the music, we were all envious, but parents and grandparents, aunts and uncles applauded with the same enthusiasm for those who could perform and those of us who couldn't do so well. We believed that life would always be like dancing with applause to keep us confident, secure, and happy. But that is not the purpose of life, we would discover.

Wilda had been married twenty-five years and had six children when the sorrow began. Her husband, Keith, died of cancer, a brain tumor. Fortunately, they had been sealed in the temple, where they had made covenants and promises that would assure an eternal binding together. She would carry on for the sake of her children. Life still had meaning and purpose, hope and promise.

She was not aware at the time that there would yet be trials and tests reaching to the very core. The subsequent years unfolded with hardly an opportunity to survive one test before another one loomed on the horizon.

According to records, there are only 100 documented families in the world and only one family in Utah—hers—who suffer from the Li-Fraumeni syndrome, a form of cancer that leaves its ravaging, destructive trail throughout the family that inherits it. Larry, Wilda's third son, was the first victim after his father died. Larry suffered from bone cancer that robbed him of his pelvic bone and entire hip socket in his teenage years. Doctors reported that he would never walk again. He told his mother in testimony, "When the brother put his hands on my head to bless me, I knew Jesus was my Brother." Larry was healed. He completed a mission and came home filled with faith and hope. He was married in the temple, anticipating a bright future, but this was not to be. His cancer returned, and still more sorrow followed when this devastating disease took the life of his son LJ at twenty-six months. Then Larry later lost his life along with his son Trevor in the boating accident mentioned above.

Wilda's fourth child and first daughter, Sharese, lived to the age of twenty-nine and had three children; then the cancer took her life. Rebecca, the younger sister, was labeled with this enemy to life at thirteen months, but she has survived. Rick, Wilda's second son, has also felt the devastating anguish of this dreaded disease. His little girl Alex has thirty-six more chemotherapy treatments to undergo in hopes of sparing her young life while fighting against the foe.

Can you imagine the heart-wrenching and faith-testing experience of looking around at those you love, with the haunting feeling that lurking in the shadows another attack may be waiting? "The Huntsman Cancer Clinic is a familiar place for us," Wilda said. "They know us; they are kind to us, and are studying our family, but that is not where I find my peace." This brave daughter of God spoke with assurance as she reported, "I'm blessed. My children were all born in the covenant. My three boys each filled an honorable mission. My children have all been endowed in the temple. We are bound as a family by temple covenants. This is not the end."

Then, changing the focus to look forward and not backward, she reported, "For the past seven years I have worked from seventy-six to eighty-one hours a week. I pay my tithing and have not had to ask for assistance. The Lord is blessing me with health to do this. I am grateful to be the mother of these children and grandchildren, whom I love with all my heart."

"Wilda," I asked, seeking further insight, "where do you get your strength, physically and spiritually?"

She said with conviction, "I know I am a daughter of God. It was shocking to me to realize I *really* am his daughter and he is my Father. Think of that! When I go to the temple to do initiatory work, I hear in my mind the promised blessing. I know who I am and who I am to become, and the same is true for my children. You can choose to wallow in self-pity, or you can look at the blue, blue sky and fluffy white clouds and know that he is there."

When the temple becomes our source of hope and promise, at the very center of our lives, we too can hold on. The Lord has spoken in times past to other Saints in their time of distress, and he speaks to each of us in our day when we learn to listen: "Ye cannot behold with your natural eyes, for the present time, the design of your God concerning those things which shall come hereafter, and the glory which shall follow after much tribulation. For after much tribulation come the blessings. Wherefore the day cometh that ye shall be crowned with much glory; the hour is not yet, but is nigh at hand" (D&C 58:3–4).

We all hope that our tests will not be like those of my cousin Wilda, but all of us will have our trials, the very ones that seem hardest for us. God will try us—not more than we can handle but also not a particle less. He will see what he can do with us. Our tests may come in the form of loneliness, disease, death, concern for a relationship, divorce, finances, unfulfilled expectations relating to the purpose of life, or just about anything else. They will come and continue, not to destroy us but to sanctify us. As the Lord has declared, "My people must be tried in all things, that they may be prepared to receive the glory that I have for them" (D&C 136:31).

I see people come to the temple day after day with heavy burdens, trials, and tests, yet they walk away with hope and promise, optimism and faith, and they leave the temple renewed. Just as in the days of Alma and his people, the Lord promises his children in our day, "I will . . . ease the burdens which are put upon your shoulders, that even you cannot feel them upon your backs, . . . and this will I do that ye may stand as witnesses for me hereafter, and that ye may know of a surety that I, the Lord God, do visit my people in their afflictions" (Mosiah 24:14).

In the temple at the close of day, when the work is done for that day and it is time to go home, I sometimes make my way slowly down the winding, three-story stairway with my hand slipping along on the smooth banister. I am reminded of my mother and the years she spent as a temple worker in this same temple in years gone by. On occasion I think I hear her voice, as in times past, but with more clarity than ever before: "And he walks with me, and he talks with me, and he tells me I am his own. And the joys we share as we tarry there, none other has ever known."

19

SWEET IS THE WORK

I know about work. Growing up on the farm, I learned about irrigating, plucking turkeys, driving a tractor, helping my dad survey for ditches, and digging postholes for fences that would be straight if you always took your sight for the next hole by lining it up with a specific target on the horizon. But none of those laborious tasks compared in my mind to the work done by our town blacksmith, Waldemar Lybbert. In his shop he labored tirelessly for long hours near an open fire, bent over the anvil welding and pounding, responding to the many needs of the village.

His large, crusty hands held the huge, heavy, iron mallet used for welding white-hot metal that would not come apart under pressure or tension of any kind. In his shop in front of the fire, wearing a heavy, dark apron and a shield over his head to protect his eyes, he could shape with intense heat and hammering whatever was needed to make or repair metal objects requested by the farmers. His work was essential to the welfare of the town during those early days. As a youth, when I thought I was dead tired from my chores, I would think of our blacksmith and decide my chores were best.

Brother Lybbert, a kind old man as I remember him, played an important role in holding our town together—not merely with his welding skills but also with his recording skills. The same hands that wielded the blacksmith's mallet also held the pen he repeatedly dipped into the small ink bottle on the desk where he sat in front of the congregation each Sunday keeping the records of ward members. As the ward clerk, he wore his white shirt each week and kept the records of births and deaths, marriages and baptisms, and even who bore their testimonies on fast Sundays.

Years later, having moved from my hometown, I had the opportunity to visit the historical department at Church headquarters in Salt Lake City, where at that time ward records were collected and filed in the archives. I was anxious to see if I could find on file some of the records of our Glenwood Ward. In the process of looking, without even a glance at the name of the ward, I immediately recognized the remarkable handwriting of our ward clerk. His flowing cursive penmanship was the standard that teachers held up to encourage their students. Brother Lybbert was a master at his work, that of welding and that of recording—an interesting combination, to say the least.

Some years ago when I received a call to *work* in the Bountiful Temple, I thought of what I had learned on the farm and from Brother Lybbert about work. I would have felt much better if I had been called to *serve* in the temple. I was not unfamiliar with getting up at 4:30 A.M., putting on worn and used work clothes, and going to work. Taking an early morning shower and donning clean, fresh clothes that would be exchanged for white clothes to go to *work* in the temple just didn't feel right. I felt it would be more respectful of the labor if one were "called to serve" in the temple rather than work in the temple.

For days, maybe weeks, as I would go to the various locations in this richly spiritual environment, assigned by the shift coordinator to stand at the door in greeting, or to help in the baptistry, the initiatory area, or the celestial room, or to be an attendant to a bride, I resisted the thought that this grand privilege might be called *work*. Helping at the cannery, yes; picking grapes at the welfare farm, yes; and certainly canning tuna fish and retaining the smell for days afterward, yes—but *working* in the temple?

One day I was sitting quietly in the celestial room, contemplating the blessings of the temple, when into my mind and my heart came a clear voice that seemed to resound through the entire room and teach me in a way I would never forget: "For behold, this is my *work* and my *glory*—to bring to pass the immortality and eternal life of man" (Moses 1:39; emphasis added).

I experienced a mighty change of thought. I was grateful to be called to work. I felt humbled to take part in His work. I wanted to work. The words of Elder John A. Widtsoe came forcibly to my mind: "In our pre-existent state, in the day of the great council, we made a certain agreement with the Almighty. The Lord proposed a plan, conceived by him. We accepted it. Since the plan is intended for all men, we became parties to the salvation of every person under that plan. We agreed, right then and there, to be not only saviors for ourselves, but measurably for the whole human family. We went into a partnership with the Lord. The working out of the plan became then not merely the Father's work, and the Savior's work, but also our work. The least of us, the humblest, is in partnership with the Almighty in achieving the purpose of the eternal plan of salvation. That places us in a very responsible attitude toward the human race" (*Utah Genealogical and Historical Magazine*, October 1943, 289).

Yes, there is work enough to do ere the sun goes down. Our work in the temples must be as tireless, steady, and unrelenting as the work of Brother Lybbert. In his blacksmith shop, he hammered together "welding links" that would withstand the greatest pressure without separating, season after season. As ward clerk, he kept a faithful record of the binding ordinances needed to weld families together on earth and in heaven.

However, the Lord's work and his glory is not accomplished in a blacksmith shop but in the temple, through the welding links of sacred ordinances that must be performed for hundreds, thousands, even millions who are depending on us to do their work. In a revelation given to the Prophet Joseph Smith regarding work for the dead, we read, "It is sufficient to know, in this case, that the earth will be smitten with a curse unless there is a welding link of some kind or other between the fathers and the children, upon some subject or other—and behold what is that subject? It is the baptism for the dead. For we without them cannot be made perfect; neither can they without us be made perfect. Neither can they nor we be made perfect without those who have died in the gospel also; for it is necessary in the ushering in of the dispensation of the fulness of times, which dispensation is now beginning to usher in, that a whole and complete and perfect union, and welding together of dispensations, and keys, and powers, and glories should take place, and be revealed from the days of Adam even to the present time" (D&C 128:18).

It is hard to imagine now that I would ever have had even the slightest concern about *working* rather than serving in the temple. It is work. No other word can be substituted.

The majesty, the grandeur, the glorious blessings of the work of this dispensation are to be felt in every mountain and valley, in every heart and soul on both sides of the veil. We catch a glimpse from the revelation given: "Let the mountains shout for joy, and all ye valleys cry aloud; and all ye seas and dry lands tell the wonders of your eternal King! And ye rivers, and brooks, and rills, flow down with gladness. Let the woods and all the trees of the field praise the Lord; and ye solid rocks weep for joy! And let the sun, moon, and the morning stars sing together, and let all the sons of God shout for joy! And let the eternal creations declare his name forever and ever! And again I say, how glorious is the voice we hear from heaven, proclaiming in our ears, glory, and salvation, and honor, and immortality, and eternal life; kingdoms, principalities, and powers!" (D&C 128:23).

Only in the temple can we present our family records wherein a welding link binds us together from one generation to the next, through time and all eternity.

Sweet is the *work*, my God, my King!

20

LEARNING
FROM SYMBOLS

As an elementary school teacher years ago, I recall the direction given by the dedicated principal of the school where I had my first teaching assignment. "Teach them to read," he said emphatically, using his hands and voice to enhance his directive. "If they don't learn to read they will remain illiterate, a tragic limitation to any opportunities for them." Although I had credentials indicating my ability to carry out this assignment and felt reasonably confident in this new experience, the manner in which this directive was given imposed a heavier burden than I had anticipated.

Racing through my mind came a review of the process for obtaining this much-needed skill. If the students entrusted to my care could recognize the letters of the alphabet, know their ABCs, and then put these symbols together to make words like *hat, cat, rat, fat,* and so on, surely this would be the beginning. They would learn to sound out the words, so-called *phonics*, but we could not stop there. Decoding the symbols to make the words was only the beginning. With words they would learn to make sentences and paragraphs, and when put together these would create stories with meaning. *Was there more?* I wondered. Yes, I knew there was more, much more.

It was in a fourth-grade reading group surrounded by a group of students that I learned a powerful lesson about comprehension. "What is the meaning of the story?" I asked as the students looked up from their books filled with symbols, words, sentences, and paragraphs. Two of the more confident students became immediately involved in a strong dispute as to the correct interpretation of the story. The symbols (letters and words) told the story of a young boy who "went to bed with the chickens." One defender of his ability to comprehend the meaning insisted, pointing to the very place on the printed page, that in fact the boy in the story slept with the chickens. He read again, with emphasis, "He went to bed with the chickens" and then elaborated with conviction, "He went out into the chicken coop and lay down with the chickens. Isn't that what it says?" The other student, just as sure of his interpretation, gave a different meaning to the symbols. "No," he insisted, "he didn't sleep with the chickens; he just went to bed early the way chickens do." The reading group took sides, defending the various interpretations of what they understood from the printed words "went to bed with the chickens."

It was time to help them understand that words are really symbols that can have layers and layers of meaning, depending on the ability of the reader to see beyond the words. "Symbols can suggest different meanings to different people," I tried to explain. "They can even mean a lot of different things to one person." A door was opening that would draw many of these students into a limitless adventure, where they would discover that the more they learn, the more there is to learn. I determined that even more important than teaching them to read was to instill in each child, if possible, an unquenchable thirst for learning, seeing beyond the symbols, grasping layers and layers of meaning.

The temple, the House of the Lord, is sometimes referred to as the "University of the Lord." In the temple I often feel like an elementary student enrolled in a graduate class. Brother Michael Wilcox explains, "We must learn how to learn in the Lord's way. In his house the method is largely symbolic, because symbols provide one of the most all-encompassing and powerful ways to learn" (*House of Glory* [Salt Lake City: Deseret Book, 1995], 17).

Learning does not come all at once but rather line upon line. During sacrament meeting one Sunday, four-year-old Jake was sitting reverently when a young deacon approached with the bread and water, sacred emblems of the sacrament. Quietly, Jake pulled his mom down so he could whisper in her ear. "Mom," he said, "tell them we don't want any, we brought our own treats." As Jake learns line upon line, he will come to see that the symbols of the bread and water represent much more: symbols of the flesh and blood of Christ; but more: the Atonement; and still more: our covenant relationship with the Savior; and more: the promise that we can always have his Spirit to be with us; and so much more. You can see the layers and layers of meaning involved when eternal truths are being learned.

And so it is with our first lessons in the temple. Elder David B. Haight counseled, "When you return [to the temple], come with an open, seeking, contrite heart, and allow the Spirit to teach you by revelation what the symbols can mean to you" (*Ensign*, May 1992, 15).

Elder John A. Widtsoe gives us great insight about

how we learn to read symbols and gradually move from elementary to graduate level in the Lord's House. He writes, "The endowment itself is symbolic: It is a series of symbols of vast realities, too vast for full understanding. Those who go through the temple and come out feeling that the service is unbeautiful have been so occupied with the outward form as to fail to understand the inner meaning. It is the meaning of the things that counts in life. . . .

"Temple worship implies a great effort of mind and concentration if we are to understand the mighty symbols that pass in review before us. Everything must be arranged to attune our ears, our minds, and our souls to the work. . . .

". . . To the man or woman who goes through the temple, with open eyes, heeding the symbols and the covenants, and making a steady, continuous effort to understand the full meaning, God speaks his word, and revelations come. The endowment is so richly symbolic. . . . It is so packed full of revelations to those who exercise their strength to seek and see, that no human words can explain or make clear the possibilities that reside in the temple service. The endowment which was given by revelation can best be understood by revelation; and to those who seek most vigorously, with pure hearts, will the revelation be greatest" (*Utah Genealogical and Historical Magazine,* April 1921, 60, 63–64).

We learn from the Prophet Joseph Smith that revelations often came to him in response to his inquiries. In the scriptures over and over we are invited to "ask, ask, ask." This is a pattern for us. A question is like a hook on the end of a fishing line. We can go fishing day after day, even wait patiently and repeat the experience time after time, but if we don't have a hook on the end of the line, all our attempts will be for naught as far as catching a fish is concerned. When we go to the temple pondering a question, we will be prepared to receive.

Enrolling at a university, a student who wishes to maximize the opportunity for learning will sometimes squeeze into an already overcrowded schedule one more class, listed in the curriculum as "effective study methods." It promises to pay big dividends.

For any who seem to be looking but not seeing the significance of their temple experience, a course outline for effective study is offered. It would include the admonition on how to awaken and arouse our faculties (see Alma 32:27). If we want to hear, we must use our ears, not our eyes. If we would see, we must use our eyes, not our nose. Just so, if we would learn things of the Spirit, we must learn through the Spirit. The Prophet Joseph described it this way: "By the power of the Spirit our eyes were opened and our understandings were enlightened, so as to see and understand the things of God" (D&C 76:12).

It must not be expected that anyone could grasp this learning by sitting in an occasional two-hour class. It will take a lifetime of regular and continuous learning, recognizing that our education will be accelerated if we don't skip classes. However, we need not be discouraged if at times our progress seems slow. To the temple we may come again and again.

In this life we may receive degrees from many institutions of higher learning, earning letters to place behind our names. But only in the temple, the university of the Lord, can we prepare ourselves to be received into the highest degree in the celestial kingdom. There we become honor students, having taken upon us his name.

21

IT FEELS SO WARM

*I*t was a bitter cold day, Tuesday, December 19, 2000. A blizzard, endangering travel, was reported in the area of Medicine Hat, about a three-hour drive north from the Cardston Alberta Temple. But this was no deterrent to Galina Demmons and her aged mother, Sofia Anohina. Early in the morning they dressed themselves warmly in coats and boots, left their home in Medicine Hat, and headed to the temple. This would be a memorable day, a day of rejoicing, a day recorded in heaven and on earth.

Sister Anohina was born in Omsk, Russia, on September 10, 1923. After two world wars, Sofia's family left their home in Russia and went to live in central Asia, in the Republic of Kyrgyzstan, which was part of the Soviet Union for seventy-three years. She was raised in a country where acknowledgment of God or any religion was prohibited. There was darkness throughout the land. When Sofia was a child, her sister, twenty years older, encouraged her with words that penetrated deep within her soul. This sister, from her own testimony and her love for her younger sister, counseled, "Go out at night, Sofia, look up at the stars, and pray to find God." The young Sofia loved and respected her sister and trusted in her counsel. She tells of going out alone at night, looking up at the starry sky, and praying to find God. Her fervent prayers were answered. She found God. But there was much more for her to find.

In March of 1998, Sofia Anohina left her home in Kyrgyzstan and arrived in Canada with a temporary visa. She was able to spend precious days with her daughter and family, who had been baptized as members of The Church of Jesus Christ of Latter-day Saints and were living in Medicine Hat, Alberta. It was there with her family that Sofia Anohina was taught the gospel and became converted. In her family circle she found God, his church, his teachings, and his people.

The following month, this elderly sister who had spent a lifetime seeking truth was lowered into the waters of baptism by one having authority. Following the baptism of water, she was confirmed and received the gift of the Holy Ghost. On that memorable day she took upon herself the name of Christ, with the promise that if she would *always* remember him and keep his commandments, she would *always* have his Spirit to be with her (see D&C 20:77).

Because of immigration restrictions and the temporary nature of her visa, Sister Anohina was not at this time permitted to stay with her daughter and family in Alberta. She must return to Kyrgyzstan and wait until official papers could be obtained for a permanent visa. She longed to be with her family, now and forever, and she had learned that this heartfelt desire could, through the gospel of Jesus Christ, one day become a reality. Regardless of existing conditions in her homeland, she would now feel an inner peace, a comfort she had not experienced previously.

Sister Anohina returned to her homeland. In her mind and in her heart she had a yearning that would not be quenched, a burning desire to receive the ordinances and covenants available only in the temple. She would be required to wait one full year following her baptism before receiving those temple ordinances. She was getting older and was anxious. After two years, Sister Anohina gained permission to leave her homeland once again and return to her family in Canada. Plans were made for her to attend the temple when she returned, there to receive the ordinances and covenants so essential to her eternal happiness.

Three weeks before the day when Sister Anohina and her daughter were to arrive at the Cardston Alberta Temple, this temple did not have the presentation and instruction available in the Russian language. Special arrangements were required that involved considerable attention. All this for a single soul? one might ask. The answer resounds in the words of President Boyd K. Packer: "Ordinances and covenants become the credentials for admission into His presence. To worthily receive them is the quest of a lifetime; to keep them thereafter is the challenge of mortality" (*Ensign*, May 1987, 22).

The day Sister Anohina arrived at the Cardston Temple with her daughter Galina, it was my privilege and honor to welcome them to the House of the Lord. I had been anticipating this important day for some time. Sister Anohina spoke only Russian and I only English. We could not communicate in words, but within minutes we shared the bonding spirit of the gospel of Jesus Christ. In our Father's house we became sisters.

With her daughter translating, I was able to give her a brief introduction. Her dark-gray, deep-set eyes, filled with the wonder of it all, radiated a joy that erased the evidence of difficult times and years of sacrifice. As I spoke with her later, this faithful daughter of God stood dressed in white, with both arms wrapped around herself, exclaiming in her native tongue words of deep gratitude that her daughter translated for me: "She says the garment is so warm, so warm." She continued embracing herself as if to retain the warmth she felt within. I'm sure she understood that the warmth she was feeling had less to do with the fabric than with the covenant. I explained, with her daughter's help, that the warmth she was experiencing was the Spirit, and it would be with her and sustain her and be a protection to her always. She would continue to feel the warmth and protection from this sacred garment she would now be privileged to wear.

After about two hours, when the temple session was completed, I met Sister Anohina and her daughter by the stairs near the entrance to the temple. They had changed into their street clothes, ready to step back out into the world, but with additional clothing that would protect them from the world. As this mother and daughter were ready to leave, Sister Anohina reached out her arms to me, embraced me, and repeated again and again words of thanks that were translated for me by the Spirit. I felt her gratitude.

Like Sister Anohina, everyone who receives the ordinances and covenants of the temple has the opportunity to feel the warmth, the protection, the tangible reminder of the blessings of the temple. The Apostle Paul, speaking of the perilous times that are a part of these last days, gave this counsel: "Take unto you the whole armour of God, that ye may be able to withstand in the evil day, and having done all, to stand" (Ephesians 6:13).

Soldiers in ancient battles wore heavy armor to serve as a protection. "However," as Elder Carlos E. Asay reminded us, "the real battles of life in our modern day will be won by those who are clad in a spiritual armor—an armor consisting of faith in God, faith in self, faith in one's cause, and faith in one's leaders. The piece of armor called the temple garment not only provides the comfort and *warmth* of a cloth covering, it also strengthens the wearer to resist temptation, fend off evil influences, and stand firmly for the right." When we leave the temple and step back out into the world, even in these perilous times, we go forth wearing "the garment as a reminder of the sacred covenants . . . made with the Lord and also as a protection against temptation and evil. *How it is worn is an outward expression of an inner commitment to follow the Savior"* (*Ensign*, August 1997, 21–22).

In August 2001 Sister Anohina, a woman of the covenant, received her permanent residence status. She would not be returning to her homeland, where laws limit freedom. She is now united with her family in Canada. Occasionally there are seasons of severe and bitter cold, with freezing temperatures that penetrate to the very core, making it hard even to breathe out of doors. Sometimes windows are frozen over, and even heavy clothing cannot provide comfort against the merciless temperatures. And yet the garment protecting her body will provide spiritual warmth, comfort, and protection—the enduring, eternal warmth found in the fire of the covenant.

22

ENDLESS, GLORIOUS YOUTH

At the very peak of the most colorful season for sunflowers one year, Heber and I were driving with some friends through the Midwest when we came upon acres of sunflowers. The beauty of the early morning light on the fields of yellow blossoms was indescribable. Deep green leaves framed the heads of these spectacular plants. Never had I seen fields so brilliant or beautiful. The plants stood tall and straight facing the morning sun. In all directions above the plants and beyond the fields, a soft light rested over the area.

Another time, in the fall of the year, our travels took us on a return trip past the very fields we had observed during that early summer season. Nothing looked the same. Instead of the bright yellow fields and the tall, straight plants, I saw only brown. The sunflowers were no longer bright with color. The leaves had fallen, and the heads of the flowers were drooping. The plants were weighed down with the heaviness of a pending harvest, bursting with fully matured seeds.

With new insight and a different perspective, I have come to realize that the process of maturing develops a different kind of beauty, one not so obvious at first. The farmer knows his crop and is quite willing, even anxious, to see the process that unfolds as one kind of beauty gives way to another. He nurtures his plants and prunes them, irrigates, and occasionally even leaves the fields without moisture for a time, thus causing the roots to reach deep into the soil. The blossoms were beautiful, but it was harvest time now. The storage bins would burst with abundance. It might be said of these sunflowers, once so bright and straight, that they had filled the measure of their creation.

In another setting, quite removed from the Midwest, this perspective returned. This time it was in the Cardston Temple as I attended a young bride just before her wedding. Her eyes were bright, with a glow of anticipation; her skin was clear, with only a hint of makeup; her hair was thick, with a healthy shine; her waist was small; the skin on her hands was soft; and her nails were beautifully manicured. She stood before the mirror in the bride's room, adding that final touch before the sacred occasion when she would be sealed for time and all eternity to a worthy young man. It was obvious that the preparation for this moment had begun years ago when she was a baby in her mother's arms. I saw in the eyes of her mother, who was standing close by, a look of gratification and maybe a question: "Where has the time gone so quickly?"

As this young woman and her eternal companion left the temple that day, stepping out into the world to begin their life together, there was radiance in the courtyard. I stood at some distance observing this happy celebration—a setting that family, friends, and cameramen try to capture on film and in their minds and hearts as well.

The day following the gathering in the courtyard, I met in a morning devotional with the sisters who had been called to serve as ordinance workers in the Cardston Temple. Walking into the room just before the meeting, I returned in thought to the lesson learned from the sunflowers. There sat each sister with the scriptures open on her lap, reading. Their bowed heads, so filled with wisdom, brought to my mind the field of mature and beautiful sunflowers. One season must pass if another is to follow. These sisters had raised their families; they no longer had children at home. They were older now and chose to spend more time in the temple. In contrast to the beauty of the young bride, I saw many hands with spots from the aging process. I saw thinning of the hair on the crown of some heads, and the shine wasn't what it once had been. Waists had widened, and some shoulders drooped. In addition to small earrings, I observed a few small hearing aids tucked into ears. Although those sisters may now have some difficulty hearing the human voice, over the years they have learned to hear the whisperings of the Spirit with increased clarity. The wrinkles that gradually encroach, first around the eyes and mouth and then on the neck and cheeks and other places, tell only part of the story. Life's rich, rewarding, challenging, and sometimes disappointing growth experiences, which over time build a solid foundation of faith and endurance, are not to be traded for the fleeting beauty of youth.

Like the sunflowers, the brilliant color of an early planting had given way to a greater purpose. That morning, without the benefit of the sun, there was evidence of heavenly light in the eyes of each of these sisters. I wondered what cosmetic counter with all its promising potions might compete even a particle with the beauty of these women bound by covenant. An inner peace radiated from their countenances, a peace that came from knowing who they were, who they are, and—because of their eternal perspective—who they are to become. In response to the question asked by Alma, I would give a reassuring yes in behalf of these sisters: "I say unto you, can ye look up to God at that day with a pure heart and clean hands? I say unto you, can you look up, having the image of God engraven upon your countenances?" (Alma 5:19).

One morning in the temple I saw the beauty of a young bride in the springtime of her life prepared to make and keep sacred covenants. The next morning I saw the radiant beauty of a full growing season, of those who had made sacred covenants, received the ordinances of the temple, and were promised through their faithfulness the blessings of exaltation.

When the time comes to report our labor in the Lord's vineyard, the harvest will be measured not by the preservation of our youth but by the preparation of our hearts and minds through a lifetime of dedicated service, unconditional love, and faithfulness to the covenants we have made.

Looking backward to the prime of youth and forward to the time of harvest, I now see beauty in both directions. I rejoice in the youthful (sometimes enviable) beauty and the promised blessings of a young bride in her season of hope, dreams, and adventure. I rejoice in the radiant countenance of those sisters who have accepted the invitation to "grow up in the Lord" and share in the lessons to be learned in the temple.

From the dedicatory prayer of the Kirtland Temple we read, "Grant, Holy Father, that all those who shall worship in this house may be taught words of wisdom. . . . And that they may grow up in thee, and receive a fulness of the Holy Ghost, and be organized according to thy laws, and be prepared to obtain every needful thing; and that this house may be a house of prayer, a house of fasting, a house of faith, a house of glory and of God, even thy house" (D&C 109:14–16). This process comes gradually as spring gives way to summer, fall, and, in the Lord's due time, the harvest.

As the Psalmist writes, "The righteous shall flourish like the palm tree: he shall grow like a cedar in Lebanon. Those that be planted in the house of the Lord shall flourish in the courts of our God. They shall still bring forth fruit in old age; they shall be fat and flourishing" (Psalm 92:12–14).

At the time of the final harvest, we have the promise that the exquisite beauty of youth and the seasoned beauty of old age will come together in a splendor we do not now comprehend.

> *How beautiful thy promise, Lord,*
> *That we may grow in truth,*
> *And live, exalted by thy word,*
> *In endless, glorious youth.*
> *With loved ones sealed in holiness*
> *By sacred temple rites,*
> *Worlds without end we may progress*
> *From heights to greater heights.*
>
> —*HYMNS, NO. 288*

ABOUT THE AUTHOR

*A*rdeth Greene Kapp served as Young Women general president in The Church of Jesus Christ of Latter-day Saints, and she later accompanied her husband in his assignment as president of the Canada Vancouver Mission. She has also served on the boards of several corporations, including Deseret Book, the Deseret News, and Utah Youth Village. A bestselling author and popular speaker, she currently serves as matron of the Calgary Alberta Temple, where her husband, Heber, is the temple president.

INDEX